KT-501-169

CRAWLEY
LEARNIN... GE
...NTRE

LEARNIN...

This boo... on or before

...er

372.
1102
ARN

WS...0294-2

Time Management

BRIGHT IDEAS

Written by Ray Arnold

Published by Scholastic Publications Ltd,
Villiers House, Clarendon Avenue,
Leamington Spa, Warwickshire CV32 5PR

© 1993 Scholastic Publications Ltd

Written by Ray Arnold
Edited by Juliet Gladston and Magdalena
Hernas
Sub-edited by Jane Wright
Illustrations by Shaun Williams
Front and back covers designed by
Anna Oliwa
Photograph by Martyn Chillmaid
Artwork by Liz Preece, Castle Graphics,
Kenilworth

Printed in Great Britain by Loxley Brothers
Ltd, Sheffield

**British Library Cataloguing in
Publication Data**
A catalogue record for this book is
available from the British Library.

ISBN 0 590 53001 1

All rights reserved. This book is sold subject to the
condition that it shall not, by way of trade or otherwise,
be lent, hired out or otherwise circulated without the
publisher's prior consent in any form of binding or
cover other than that in which it is published and
without a similar condition, including this condition,
being imposed upon the subsequent purchaser.

No part of this publication may be reproduced, stored
in a retrieval system, or transmitted, in any form or by
any means, electronic, mechanical, photocopying,
recording or otherwise, without the prior permission of
the publisher, except where photocopying for
educational purposes within a school or other
educational establishment is expressly permitted in the
text.

Contents

– 6 FEB 1997

UNIVERSITY OF CHICHESTER
BOGNOR REGIS CAMPUS
UPPER BOGNOR ROAD
BOGNOR REGIS
WEST SUSSEX
PO21 1HR

4

Introduction

This book is about the practical management of time. It is directed specifically at the classroom teacher and is intended to give guidance, not theory. Many of the suggested activities can be carried out by the individual teacher, but there is also a substantial section in Chapter 3 on working with colleagues. This is especially relevant since so many schools now plan collaboratively, especially with respect to the National Curriculum requirements.

Virtually all teachers agree that time is a very scarce resource. We talk about 'making time', but in reality this is one thing we cannot do. We can waste it, use it, organise it and prioritise it in various ways, but we cannot make it, store it or stop it. Time passes whatever we do. Teachers are very aware of this in the education of children. In terms of time passing, there is never a second chance – a child will never again be four-and-a-half or ten-and-a-quarter. Each wasted moment can never be reclaimed. Although we cannot make more time, we can learn to organise and manage it so that we can achieve more in the time available.

It is worth remembering how little time children actually spend in school. Even when in school, not all that time is lesson time. If we assume an average of about five contact hours a day and 200 days a year at school, primary school children spend less than 12 per cent of their lives in school lesson time, even assuming 100 per cent attendance. To put it another way, classroom hours in the whole of the seven years of compulsory primary schooling amount to less than 42 weeks! However, despite this short time, there is no doubt about the difference school can make to learning outcomes – look at the vast amount of research that has been done on effective schools, for example, the ILEA Junior School Survey, *School Matters*, (1988) to name but one.

It is hardly surprising, therefore, that teachers feel tremendous time pressures on both themselves and their pupils. These are considered perhaps the most difficult aspect of their job and can be the cause of a great deal of stress. The demands of the National Curriculum and its assessment arrangements are particularly challenging

in terms of time. The legal requirement to spend a 'reasonable amount' of time on each curriculum area, even though this can be partly met through integrated work, means that teachers need to manage their time with great care. The assessment of pupil learning is now much more of a formal process, with achievement having to be recorded and reported to an extent never before required. In every way the management of time has become a key issue for all teachers, and specific support and advice in this area is now crucial.

Managing these scarce contact hours with pupils is the central theme of this book. Management in this sense means organisation and deployment of time so as to promote the most effective learning for all pupils. Ill-managed time will easily tick away, wasting learning opportunities. There may, of course, be other opportunities but the actual time has been lost for ever. This is not to say that all learning is planned and intended; but the teacher who organises time carefully is going to be in a better position to make effective use of both planned and unplanned opportunities for learning.

Personal organisation

The teacher who manages her own time effectively is undoubtedly going to be better at managing the curriculum and promoting learning as a result. Therefore, the starting point for effective time management should be personal organisation.

This chapter is concerned with practical ways in which the busy class teacher can save time through better personal organisation and increased awareness of time issues. The suggestions are based on making more efficient use of the time available rather than constantly extending the number of hours worked. Of course, every professional teacher accepts that some work has to be done out of school hours – however, it is not beneficial to either her or her pupils for a teacher to exhaust herself through overwork. Being the teacher of a lively class is quite exhausting enough!

The suggested activities are intended for the individual teacher, but there is certainly some value in getting the help and advice of another colleague, especially with the discussion of time-log information. This will also be useful preparation for some of the following chapters which involve enlisting the active co-operation of others.

A time analysis

Objective
To provide information about actual lesson time.

What you need
Photocopiable page 99.

What to do
In order to make the best use of your working hours, examine how you spend them now. As a first step, try looking at a fairly substantial block of time such as a whole school week.

Complete the grid on photocopiable page 99 to work out the actual lesson time that your class has in a typical school week.

Are you amazed/horrified/not surprised by what you have discovered? One interesting and valuable way of analysing the information in the chart is to classify it in two ways – things that you as an individual can do something about, and those which require collective action by the staff. It is important to do something with the information – my reaction, after the initial shock when I did this analysis, was to be really punctual arriving back to class after play and lunch times. This communicated itself to the children, who also came back promptly, expecting to see me there and ready to work straight away!

If the grid shows a number of people dropping in for no particular reason, there is no harm in letting them know tactfully that lunch or break times might be better for that quick word. Having a reputation for not welcoming unnecessary interruptions while you are teaching is a valuable asset!

Collective action is sometimes the only answer. If you are plagued by teacher messages, especially those sent via a pupil, you need a collective agreement to do something different, perhaps a whiteboard with markers in the staffroom. Pointing out the time out of lessons for the messenger is often salutary.

Dinner money routines are another potential time-waster. Ideally, they should be handled out of class but teachers can minimise the time needed. Fill the book in promptly as the children come in (or, better still, use a classroom helper if you have one) and get it off to the

office – do not let latecomers force you to readjust and retotal! If possible, let the children do it as a useful maths exercise. Do not ever delegate the class attendance register to the children, however – this is a legal document and should be handled by you alone.

An out-of-class time-log

Objective
To provide information about the time spent on schoolwork outside class hours.

What you need
Photocopiable page 100.

What to do
Keep a personal log for a week of how you use your out-of-class work time. The log should include all the time spent working, including work at home, as well as meetings, preparation, post-holder work and so on, carried out at school. This can be grouped by category if you find it helpful, for example, preparation, marking, record-keeping, collaborative planning, post-holder work, mounting and displaying work, meetings, school clubs and so on. Try not to choose more than five or six categories for your log. It is a waste of time to do this in great detail, so do not be afraid to estimate or to categorise quickly and code your categories for ease of reference. It helps to jot down notes in the middle and at the end of the day and categorise them at the end of the week, but do whatever suits you best. You may also find it helpful to use photocopiable page 100.

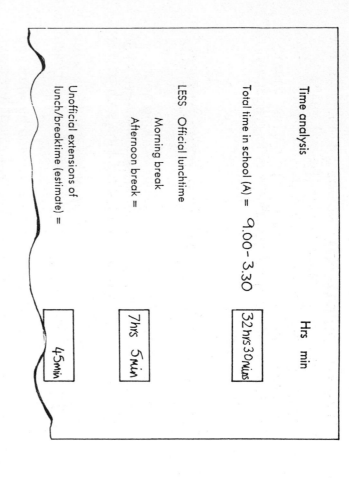

Time analysis	Hrs	min
Total time in school (A) = 9.00–3.30	32 hrs 30 mins
LESS Official lunchtime		
Morning break =	7 hrs 5 min
Afternoon break =	
Unofficial extensions of lunch/breaktime (estimate) =	45 min

However, analysis is only valuable if it leads to action of some kind, for example, training the children to mount their work, focusing on key pupil learning in the record-keeping and cutting down on marginal detail. Therefore, make sure that you use your log regularly.

The urgent and the important

Objective
To make a distinction between what is urgent and what is important and to apply it in prioritising tasks.

What you need
A list of your current priorities.

What to do
There are, unfortunately, quite a few people who show in the practical management of their everyday lives that they do not distinguish between the urgent and the important. Here are four possible categories which will help you make the distinction.
● Urgent (but not important): everyday things demanding prompt action. These create pressure to act immediately and, indeed, many children (and adults, too!) are adept at making their immediate need into an urgent priority. In the context of the classroom, simple rules such as 'put up your hand if you need my help' will prevent a flood of requests for urgent attention. (See 'Queueing at your desk', page 42.) As part of your long-term strategy, teach the children that a measure of independent action, for example, attempting to spell an unfamiliar word rather than asking you about the correct spelling, is rewarded.

The important thing about this exercise is to be as honest and factual as possible – after all, this information is private and intended to be useful to you alone.

Take a long, hard look at the information you have gathered. Perhaps you do a lot of mounting and displaying work – could the children do more of it? Is there something that you feel you ought to do more of?

The time you spend reflecting on the information you have gathered is time well spent. For example, what balance do you strike between preparation and record-keeping? Are you spending more time in administrative-type meetings than in collaborative planning with colleagues? Make links with what you do in school: do you spend as much time on work out of class as you do in class? Many teachers work fifty hours a week. Is this reasonable – how much of your out-of-class time has a direct influence on what you do in the classroom?

Out-of-class time-log

Possible categories might be: preparation, marking, reading, record-keeping, collaborative planning, postholder work, mounting and displaying work, meetings, school clubs, etc. – try to have no more than five or six categories for your log. Another way of using the log is to write a short description of your out-of-school activities for each day and estimate how long they take.

Total out-of-class/out-of-school hours	21½ hrs

		Hours worked
Mon	①–1½ hrs ②–1 hr ③–2 hrs ⑥–1 hr - Put up a large display	5½
Tue	①–1 hr ③ 1 hr ⑥–inset session 1½ hrs.	3½
Wed	①–1 hr ⑤ 1 hr ④–1½ hrs	3½
Thu	①–1 hr ⑥–3 hrs Took a group to the theatre	4
Fri	③–½ hr ①½ hr	1
Sat	None!	0
Sun	①–2 hrs	2

With adults, learn to say 'I'm sorry but I can't deal with it now'. It is much better than rushing to deal with someone else's urgent request or ignoring your own priorities.

● Important (but not urgent): matters of great significance, especially those concerning children and their learning. These include developmental and long-term issues such as children's increasing grasp of abstract concepts or collaborative planning in a year team. As these do not necessarily need immediate attention, things in the 'Urgent' category often take precedence. If you have identified something as 'Important' make sure you allow enough time to deal with it.

● Urgent and important: safety matters belong in this category, as do situations when children are at a particularly receptive stage of the learning process. However, this combination is rarer than you think and confusing the two categories leads to problems in time management.

● Neither urgent nor important: all the classroom and out-of-classroom trivia belong here. All of us spend some time doing things which do not really matter, to the exclusion of those that do. This is known as 'displacement activity' – we defer an important but perhaps difficult task in favour of a familiar, if trivial one. For instance, we might put off reorganising the book corner but prepare yet another worksheet.

Bearing in mind the above categories, the following analysis might be useful in making the necessary practical distinctions.

● Is this 'urgent' matter really urgent?
● How do I decide this – what reasons are there?
● What follows if I do not deal with it?
● Will my children suffer in any way?

Repeat the process with something you would say was important.

The next stage is to ask 'How urgent, how important?' Give the items on your to do list a mark out of 5 for both urgency and importance. Anything with a total score of 10 should have been done yesterday! Anything with a score of 2 should come off the 'To do' list immediately.

Prioritisation

Objective
To establish clear priorities which make for effective teaching.

What you need
A list of things you would like to get done the next day.

What to do
The previous activity highlighted the distinction between the urgent and the important as a necessary preliminary to effective prioritisation. Use this distinction to help you prioritise.

Look ahead to the next day and make a brief list of things you would like to get done in that day. These priorities could be personal or classroom ones, but they need to be short-term and specific. Classify each one in the following way, using the appropriate letter.

A – I must do this today.
B – I should do this today.
C – I would like to do this today.

The six Ws

Objective

To provide an easily remembered framework which helps you to work systematically.

What you need

No special requirements.

What to do

In real life we often do not have the time for systematic problem solving – something always needs doing yesterday! However, in every time management tool-kit there should be a way of systematically approaching larger problems. The following 'six Ws' will help you tackle new or difficult tasks.

You might end up with a list coded as follows:

- Make sure the whole class finish their book reviews (A).
- Work with a small group on a group writing activity (B).
- See the headteacher about a class visit (C).
- Put up the new display in the book corner (C).
- Finish a special-needs report form (A).
- Start a group on a science investigation (B).

You should aim to deal with at least the A-rated matters, moving on to the Bs if time permits and so on.

Follow-up

This method can be adapted in a number of ways. For instance, you might have a time priority code such as the following:

A – tomorrow;
B – this week;
C – next week;
D – this month; and so on.

- WHAT is the problem or what do you want to do? Be clear!
- WHY are you doing, or trying to solve, this? (If there is no good reason, don't bother!)
- WHO is going to be involved or needs to be consulted?
- WHEN does it need to happen?
- WHERE is it going to happen?
- WHICH WAY? Make a plan using answers to the above questions.

This framework, as well as being a time-saver for the individual, can also be used by the whole staff or a small planning group as a systematic approach to a task.

Here is an example of how the six Ws can help solve a concrete task.

- WHAT: I want to reorganise the book corner.
- WHY: displays are messy; children can't get at the books easily; the seating is inadequate; I can't monitor what's happening there easily.
- WHO: me mostly, but the language post-holder said she would give advice and Marion next door has offered to help with rearranging the books. Children to help as well.

- WHEN: Thursday after school and I can finish off the display with a group of children Friday lunchtime.
- WHERE: in the right-hand corner of the classroom close to my desk.
- WHICH WAY: Start with a sketch of the proposed layout. Some small tables need shifting – check with Marion when she could help. Set aside some books for repair. Carpet needs moving – ask the caretaker. Must make new notices.

Will a computer help me?

Objective

To assess whether your work-load and the sorts of tasks you do are suitable for computer assistance.

What you need

A brief written description or summary of your work-load and main tasks.

What to do

As someone who came late to personal use of a computer after years of scepticism, I feel qualified to talk with some realism about the time-saving aspects of using one. I now find a computer indispensable but only for some tasks – there are many things I do which would be done more slowly if I used a computer. Let's look at what computers are good at.

- They are good at doing complex calculations very quickly; for instance allowing you to see the effects of changing one figure, say in a budget, by rapidly re-calculating all the other figures affected by that change (the spreadsheet function). If you have such a programme, it could be used for keeping track of the contributions, expenses and balances of a school journey, where contributions come in irregularly and where it is important to know the financial position at any time. A spreadsheet could also be useful for keeping track of your post-holder's budget. However, the dinner money is best done using pencil and paper, with perhaps a small calculator to help you.

• Computers are useful for producing documents and lists which need to be updated or changed frequently. A draft policy, for instance, if entered on a computer, can go through a whole series of consultations with changes at each stage made very simply, saving hours of work. Class lists sorted alphabetically or by date of birth are very useful to the class teacher and names can be added or deleted easily.

• It is a good idea to have some standard templates on a computer for routine letters and communications. Virtually all word-processing software allows you to create a standard document, set up the way you want it, for example, a letter to parents asking the reason for a child's absence. Every time you need to send such a letter you can call it up, make the necessary changes and save/print it. The original template remains intact for you to use again.

• If your software has the database function, you can use your computer to store large amounts of information sorted in a variety of ways. It can take a long time to set up your database, but once you have done that, tasks such as pupil profiling, for instance, become much easier. However, you may find that a loose-leaf book and a card index are more accessible since they need less setting up. Of course, records for the whole school are a different story, but remember that information on pupils stored on computer is subject to the 1989 Data Protection Act and is accessible to parents.

• Certain types of computers and printers, particularly laser printers, give excellent standards of presentation, often indistinguishable from commercially produced material. The increasing number of teachers who have access to such equipment can enhance their pupils' learning through imaginatively produced curriculum materials. It is a good idea to produce resource materials rather than worksheets designed for one-time use. Examples of such materials include the following:

• a resource pack of the immediate neighbourhood (indispensable for National Curriculum History and Geography);
• a set of maps – scanned in or from a programme;
• a school/class anthology of favourite poetry.

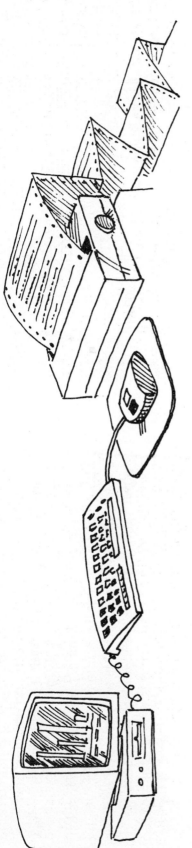

Drafting documents on the computer

Objective

To save time by using a computer to produce draft documents.

What you need

A computer and printer with word-processing software.

What to do

A computer is a great time-saver for processing documents which need updating and re-drafting. You might, for instance, be working on a draft language policy. If you use a computer for your draft, you can easily incorporate any changes suggested in subsequent staff consultations.

Follow-up

Some schools are reluctant to review policy documents regularly, not because they are complacent but because they are reluctant physically to rewrite them each time. A computer really does make such tasks much easier and saves a lot of time. It is also easy to save the original version to come back to if necessary, without having to store earlier drafts in paper form.

Computer templates

Objective

To save time by using computer templates for forms and returns that you need to fill in regularly.

What you need

A computer and printer – most word-processing software will enable you to make templates. You will also find templates in *Teacher Timesavers: Essentials for everyday*, Pat Gooch (1992) Scholastic.

What to do

There is some danger of using computer technology for work which may be better done using pen and paper. Therefore, before you embark on creating new templates, ask yourself, 'Will it really save me time?' (see 'Will a computer help me?' page 12).

The most useful template is probably the class list, with a space against the name of each child, which can be printed out as needed. It is easy to insert additional names and to change the layout of your template, if necessary. A spreadsheet grid is very useful for creating this type of list – just enter names, instead of figures, into the grid spaces.

Task batching

Objective

To save time by grouping similar tasks together until enough have been collected to justify an allocation of time to deal with them.

What you need

A simple classification/recording sheet such as the one on photocopiable page 101.

What to do

It is often not a good use of time to do a particular task immediately, especially if you know that meanwhile you will accumulate a number of similar tasks. Therefore, waiting until you have a number of similar tasks to do and planning to do them together can be very time-efficient.

Decide on three or four main categories of work which recur frequently and which seem to take up substantial amounts of time when done as they arise (this needs thought; some things are best done, or have to be done, immediately).

It is usually possible to 'lock' the template to prevent accidental changes. Whatever changes you want to make are entered on a copy of your original template, thus preserving the original for further use.

Another useful template to have is an annual report form. You can fill in the details for each child 'on screen' using the same template and save each report separately. You could, of course, print the template out and complete it by hand.

Here are some other ideas for templates:
● a certificate of achievement/good behaviour – very popular with children, especially as they can take them home;
● a request form for parental help of various kinds (see page 117);
● a pupil self-assessment template which the children could fill in on the screen, then print out and file in a work folder (see page 111);
● a school magazine template (if your software has a page layout programme);

A word of warning: do not be tempted to use any of those programmes which provide a set of stock words and phrases for report writing. They 'save' time in the wrong way!

Here are some possible categories:

- non-urgent correspondence;
- points to raise with colleagues;
- a major task, such as planning an assembly;
- updating individual records.

Record the categories on photocopiable page 101 and enter, with the date, each task as it arises. When you have the time, deal with a block of tasks and strike them out as they are completed.

Follow-up

This batching of tasks can usefully be carried over into collaborative planning sessions with, for example, a year-group team of teachers looking at such tasks together and planning how and when they might best be managed.

People to contact	Done	Things to write	Done	Things to obtain	Done	Other tasks	Done
School Journey letter for Mrs Jones (parent of Hannah)	11/6/92	Report for Educ. Psychologist Note to Mr Berry (Hughes)	6/6/92	Books for next terms topic. Batteries for the electricity pack. Goldfish food!	9/6/92	Weekly forecast for Head.	7/6/92
Gavin Company (quotes for outing)		Museum Education Dept - confirm visit in writing.		* A plant to invigorate up library area send for inspection copy of Geography Scheme.	9/6/92 9/6/92	Duplicate school journey clothing list. Car in for servicing, get lift from Margot	8/6/92
Deputy Head - can she help with basic workshop?	10/6/92	Final letter to parents about school journey.	8/6/92				
School keeper - to mend our cupboard	• Do these together		* Do these sat am.		* Do these together		

Knowing the right time

Objective

To know at all times in the classroom what the precise time is.

What you need

A large quartz kitchen clock.

What to do

It is important for the class teacher to know exactly what the time is throughout the day. Most classroom clocks are inaccurate and some do not even pretend to give an approximation of the correct time. Quite apart from the punctuality aspects, it is important to know the correct time as, for example, there can be legal implications of allowing children to go home early. The purchase and display of a quartz kitchen clock will give class teachers an accurate time check and will save a lot of unnecessary anxiety, as well as time.

It is a good idea to involve the children in checking the time. A chiming clock would help to make them aware of passing hours. You might also like to wear a large, prominent analogue watch for the same reason. Try using a simple kitchen timer in the classroom: for example, brief a small group of children to spend 25 minutes researching a topic in the library or 15 minutes reading quietly.

Follow-up

Access to accurate timekeeping is a whole-school issue. All classrooms should have accurate quartz clocks and so should the hall, libraries and group rooms. The best and biggest clock should be in the staffroom!

Being on time

Objective
To utilise class contact time fully.

What you need
An accurate watch.

What to do
Make it an unvarying habit to be in the classroom before the children arrive. If you collect the children from the playground, be there well in time. This apparently simple routine has major benefits in terms of how other colleagues and the children regard you, as well as being very much in the interests of the children who get no second chances in terms of lost learning time.

Having a reputation for punctuality when it matters is of enormous value to a teacher. There are so many opportunities to gain such a reputation, ranging from arrival at assemblies through to handing in a return on time, and likewise many chances to lose it!

Children are usually very interested in time and its measurement, so why not enlist their help in managing time and being punctual? For example, let them take it in turns to measure some of the 'wasted time' lost when travelling round the school, changing for PE and so on, using a stop-watch; let them also make suggestions for how to waste less time. If they see a purpose to, for example, not talking while going to assembly, they will keep the rule much more readily.

Follow-up
The following activity will help to focus on these opportunities.

A punctuality audit

Objective
To help you assess how punctual you are and review your attitudes to time-keeping.

What you need
Photocopiable page 102, stop-watches or timer clocks.

What to do
Not many of us realise how much time we lose in the course of a working week through being unpunctual, if only occasionally. Likewise, many of us are unaware of the conflict between our professed and real attitudes to punctuality.

Complete the punctuality audit on photocopiable page 102. Be honest or there is no point filling the chart! The results should give you some food for thought. Are you really as punctual as you believe yourself to

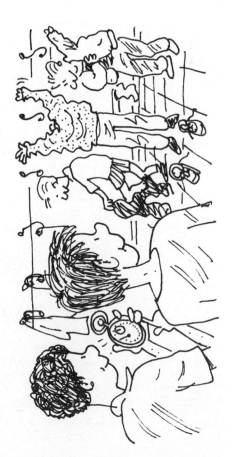

What does a ghost get at the opticians? SPOOKTACLES!

---

be? Are there particular days/times when you are likely to be late? Try to use your insights to achieve an improvement in your time-keeping and to change your attitude, to reflect the best interests of the children and their learning.

Follow-up

It could be both fun and useful to enlist the children's co-operation in keeping good time. You might like to try some of the following:

● Arrange a favourite activity, such as a 5-minute joke-telling session, for immediately after breaks.

● Write daily activities on a poster or notice-board. At the beginning of each day, go through the list, explaining to the children what time each activity will begin and how long it will take. This exercise helps children to take responsibility for knowing what is on the agenda.

● Give the issue a bit of a competitive edge – children love to compete with their teacher! Who will be there first after the whistle blows to collect the class from the playground? Does the class have to wait for the teacher or is it the other way round?

● Make it clear to the parents and the children that the classroom is open 15 minutes early in the morning.

Planning for the unexpected

Objective

To make planned provision for unplanned developments in a specific project.

What to do

Most planning does not make deliberate provision for unexpected occurrences. Why, then, should we plan for something we cannot foresee?

With most major school events, such as outings, performances or preparation of a policy, it is wise to build in extra time at the planning stage. Given that they involve a large number of children and adults, and external and unpredictable factors such as weather and public transport, something is bound to happen to call for a time cushion. Just how much time to allow depends on the particular event, but a time cushion of about 10 per cent is usually about right. For example, if a series of staff meetings is planned, it is worth scheduling an extra one to cope with any overrun.

TIME CUSHIONS

Follow-up

Collaborative planning in this area is very helpful in achieving realistic prediction. Use your colleagues' expertise to aid your time-planning.

Sorting out the mess

Objective
To make a start on coping with a mountain of paper.

What you need
An A4 plastic file, a box file, a sturdy box, some plastic carrier bags.

What to do
There is nothing more disheartening than having a mountain of paper around the classroom 'because I might need it one day'. If all else fails and you have accumulated such a mountain, try the following.

Clear all the papers off your desk and empty the drawers into a large box. Don't panic — nothing has been thrown away yet! Put anything you know you must keep in the A4 plastic folder — if there is more than a page or two, put it in the box file. Put the rest, and it should be the majority, into the plastic carrier bags. Stack the bags neatly in a cupboard as a 'holding area'.

Nearly always, you will find that you do not need anything in the bags. If by some chance you really need something, you can rummage through them. After a month or so you can dispose of the contents without feeling guilty. (This treatment is not recommended for National Curriculum documents, however much you may be tempted!)

'This week' file

Objective
To save time by collecting material related to the activities of the current week.

What you need
An A4 plastic folder or pocket file.

What to do
Having a 'This week' file which has to be cleared at the end of each week can be a time-effective method of prioritising. It ensures that tasks are not carried over endlessly, week after week.

Create a 'This week' file and label it clearly. An A4 plastic folder is quite adequate and easy to carry around and store. Put in it anything that you know you will need to deal with or that relates to activities in which you are involved this week.

This folder is intended to be used for administrative or related matters and it is probably best to have a separate system for your teaching plans and notes. The

Storage of work in progress

Objective
To keep whatever you are currently working on in an easily visible and accessible form.

What you need
A plastic A4 storage folder, a few paper-clips, a current piece of work in progress.

What to do
In contrast to a 'This week' file (see page 19), a 'Work in progress' folder should contain material related to only one thing. If you are working on one particular fairly substantial matter, for example, an extended report on a folder might contain letters to reply to, a meeting agenda, a photocopied article to read, brief notes of your own and so on. It is important, if you have such a file, to clear it at the end of the week and not use it as a holding file for anything you did not have time to deal with! Let an item stay in the file for the next week only in the most exceptional circumstances.

Follow-up
Try to develop sensible strategies for removing the actual material from the file after you have dealt with it. Keep your own brief notes of an article and pass on the photocopy, throw out your scribbles once they have served their purpose, get rid of letters and memos once you have replied to them, unless they are important enough to keep.

child, a staff discussion paper or an administrative task such as organising some aspect of a school fête, keep all the bits and pieces related to this in one A4 file. Use the paper-clips to group related pieces of paper. You will save hours hunting around for vital bits of paper if you immediately put anything you do or receive that is related to the task into the folder. Keep it accessible in a bag, briefcase or in an uncluttered drawer and remember, when the task is finished, clear it out!

Do not be tempted to open dozens of these files whenever something comes up. Use a 'This week' file for the specific short-term matters. Try not to have more than two major tasks on the go at once, but perhaps for busy teachers this is too much to hope!

A personal organiser

Objective
To make time-saving use of the flexible page format of a personal organiser.

What you need
A personal organiser with diary pages. The 'week on two pages' kind is recommended. The 'week on one page' diaries are very restrictive and the 'one page a day' versions are much too bulky and cumbersome to use effectively.

What to do
Interleave the diary pages with either blank sheets or the specially printed 'To do' sheets (the former are more flexible). Try to have no more than one blank sheet per week. You can use these sheets to make notes on or to compile lists and so on.

You might, for instance, write detailed notes of how you are going to organise the class outing on the sheet immediately next to the diary entry. Anything associated with a diary entry can go on a sheet, avoiding scribbled notes in the tight diary spaces or hunting for a scrap of paper on which you wrote some vital piece of information.

Follow-up
A personal organiser, despite its somewhat unfortunate image, is a very useful and under-used time-saving tool. Its flexible format allows the user to arrange, remove and add pages at will. Some teachers keep a sheet for each child and jot down classroom observation notes, which can then be easily removed and stored. Others keep 'logs' of main learning points on courses or visits to other schools which are immediately available for reference.

A 'Bring forward' file

Objective

To ensure appropriate action is taken in time.

What you need

A clear plastic A4 wallet, an A4 contents sheet (see photocopiable page 103).

What to do

Memory can be unreliable in reminding you what needs to be done and when. The function of a 'Bring forward' file is to alert you to action that needs taking at a certain time based on previous action on received information. The file is designed to provide the information you need to take the right action at the right time.

Label your clear wallet 'Bring forward' and put in it a copy of photocopiable page 103. When you receive a document or any other information for which you will have a specific future use, or will need to action on a specific date, write at the top of it the date on which action is needed. Then file it in your wallet in chronological order. At the same time, enter the appropriate details on the contents page, so that it is immediately visible when you pick up the file.

Bring forward file

Contents

Date	Document	Action needed
2 Feb	Items for agenda for Language policy meeting	Plan and distribute final agenda
9 Feb	Agenda for Language	Take to meeting

For example, if you have sent a letter to Mrs Jones asking for a reply by 12 March, put a copy of that letter into your file with '12 March' written at the top. Fill in the contents sheet as shown in the example below. This will remind you to check, on 12 March, whether a reply has been received and, if not, to chase it up.

Do not use this file for just anything you think might be useful generally; keep it for what you know you will need at a particular time. Ensure that you check the contents page at the start of every day. It is important that the date must not pass without the item being actioned, and re-entered if necessary.

A basic equipment kit

Objective

To save time by labelling small equipment and keeping it in a container.

What you need

A sturdy and fairly large fabric pencil-case (plastic ones are much less satisfactory) or a cloth bag with a draw-string. The latter can be conveniently hung in various places in the classroom, but can be a nuisance if too big.

What to do

Many teachers waste a lot of time trying to locate essential items of stationery and small pieces of equipment. The frustration and disruption this causes is stressful as well as time-wasting and it is worth doing something about this. Make a list of all the essential items you need during the course of the day. Collect a set of all these items and mark your name clearly on each one, no matter how small or cheap the object. No colleague will casually take something which is so marked and your children need to recognise instantly that the item belongs to you and therefore needs returning fast. Most children will respect these items and compete to return them to you if you leave them about.

Your list might include red and black biros and felt-tipped pens, an eraser, paper-clips, a miniature stapler, adhesive stick, a 'Post-It' pack, Blu-Tack and so on.

Follow-up

The principle of marking your own equipment and actively enlisting the help and co-operation of your children in respecting their property as well as yours can be applied and extended in all sorts of ways. For example, make a small group of children responsible for their own set of equipment, such as felt-tipped pens, rulers and adhesive. They should then code this equipment using different-coloured and shaped self-adhesive labels.

Setting up a year planner

Objective

To save time by planning ahead for the school year.

What you need

A year planner, a pack of stickers of different shapes, colours and sizes.

What to do

Year planners, which are sometimes given away free by educational magazines and equipment distributors, can be a useful time-saver in a number of ways. As well as functioning as a diary, they allow instant visual checks of available dates, the number of days to go before an event (including holidays) and they are, of course, invaluable for planning. Used properly, they are an excellent teaching aid. For example, they are very useful for helping children to develop the concept of a week and a month through visual experience. How many weeks to Christmas? What is the longest term? How many weeks to Ranjit's birthday? When shall we book the coach for the outing?

Decide what different kinds of information you want to display and use the different-coloured and shaped stickers to present the different types of information. To really save time, you need to be able to glance at the planner and get immediate visual information. Do not write directly on the planner – it looks messy and you can't make changes easily. Write something on the sticker if you need to. INSET days, staff and planning meetings, class assemblies, school journeys, outings and concerts and class visitors are all possibilities for the planner.

Follow-up

Involving the children in using and referring to the class year planner can be very rewarding. Most children like information displayed like this; when they can see that it is all about their, and their teacher's, activities the planner can become an educationally valuable tool.

Do it now!

Objective

To promote doing something you have to do sooner rather than later.

What you need

No special requirements.

What to do

If you have a form to fill in or a report to write, do it now! The great majority of such tasks can be dispatched in less than 15 minutes, but leaving them to accumulate can make them appear more daunting than they really are. More than half the stress brought about by paperwork is caused by *thinking* about how much you have to do rather than *doing* it. Having a reputation among the staff for getting things done yesterday is

great for morale and will see you through the odd spell when you feel exhausted, cannot be bothered or just forget.

Think of something you need to do, but which you least wish to do, then think how good you would feel if you had done it. It might motivate you to go and do it!

Follow-up

Set aside a regular 10 minutes every day for small administrative tasks. Setting a timer and making yourself a cup of coffee might aid your motivation to get them done.

Using time-scraps

Objective
To make productive use of short periods of time.

What you need
Some reflection on the time-scraps in your professional life.

What to do

Time-scraps are short periods of unused time which every professional has in the course of her work. It does *not* include proper breaks for lunch and morning coffee which are time spent well. However, there are often the odd five- and ten-minute periods, both in and out of the classroom, which could perhaps be used to more purpose. Try to analyse where these might occur and see if you could use them for something specific.

You can create time-scraps by, for example, being very punctual when class sessions start or deliberately speeding up routines such as registration. The time saved really does add up!

Here are some examples of time-scraps:
- waiting for a train;
- waiting for a meeting to start;
- singing practice;
- rehearsals;
- children working silently . . .

. . . and some suggestions for using them:
- reviewing individual children;
- organising your thoughts for the beginning of the day;
- planning a school trip;
- a brief word with a colleague;
- writing a note;
- making a business phone call;
- setting up the video or the radio.

It is best to use time-scraps for relatively small tasks, which can be completed in under ten minutes.

Speed reading

Objective
To increase your productive reading speed by using a scanning technique.

What you need
A page of unfamiliar text; somebody to ask you questions.

What to do
Fluent readers do not read every word. Instead, they scan a piece of text in sections, looking for meaning and doing a great deal of predicting of what lies ahead. Only if something unexpected or unpredictable happens, does the rapid reader slow down or stop and reread a passage. It is possible to increase reading speed considerably by consciously practising this scanning technique and focusing on the meaning or gist of the text rather than each individual word. This is the central principle of all those speed-reading courses.

One specific technique is to look at a previously unseen page of text for an exactly measured period of time, say, 20 seconds, and then see if you can answer questions about it asked by someone familiar with the text. Just scan the whole page rapidly a couple of times, including a top-to-bottom scan, as well as a left-to-right scan. You will be surprised at how much you can absorb in such a short time and how much you can improve through practice.

Children mounting and displaying their own work

Objective
To save time by developing children's skills in mounting and displaying their own work.

What you need
A medium-sized Rotatrim (a very safe and easy to use rotary guillotine), a variety of mounting paper, a range of adhesives, a specific area in the class for mounting work.

What to do
There are no short cuts in teaching children how to mount and display their own work, but once some of them are confident, they can be involved in helping others (see 'Teaching pairs' on page 41). A Rotatrim or similar is essential as traditional guillotines, even those with guards, are completely unsafe for children to use, even under close supervision. Children should mount their work in class time, during the short periods of time which might not otherwise be used productively. There have to be clear routines established for access to the necessary materials and space to do the work. Again, the principle is to save time in the long-term by using it intensively at the outset to establish and reinforce what is required.

It is possible to train quite young children to mount their work and, as they get older, the quality of the finished products should improve. Alongside the 'technical' aspects of mounting work should go a programme for raising awareness of the aesthetic issues involved and also the purposes of display, including the social ones, for example, the importance of valuing the work of everybody in the class. Unless this happens, children, who might be very competent at mounting their own work, cannot adequately contribute to how a display should look and whose work should be represented.

An ideas book

Objective
To record immediately anything you feel might be useful.

What you need
A small hardback notebook suitable for a handbag or jacket pocket.

What to do
This idea has a very long history. King Alfred was said to have owned such a book, where he recorded all sorts of things which he found striking, amusing or useful. Clearly, he did not jot down cake recipes!

The first thing to do is to remember to carry the notebook with you at all times. Good ideas can occur at unexpected times and places, for example, a shop window can inspire a new plan for classroom displays. If you have such a notebook handy, you will be able to trace ideas and references much more quickly than if you jotted them down on scraps of paper and old envelopes.

You might like to use your notebook as King Alfred did, to write down anything that attracts your attention, not only classroom ideas: quotes, jokes, poems and so on. Try using the following headings in your notebook:

- Teaching/classroom organisation ideas;
- Resources;
- Places to visit/things to see;
- Quotes/poems/jokes;
- Children's books;
- Visual/artistic ideas;
- Ideas for problem-solving tasks.

Follow-up
If you find that you have been making a lot of notes under particular headings, you might like to start separate specialised notebooks.

I must get him a personal organiser for Xmas

A course and professional reading log

Objective

To provide a record of the main learning points and reflections on training courses and professional reading.

What you need

A small hardbound notebook (about 20.5cm by 15cm is ideal). Plain paper is the most flexible since it is easier to sketch on. Alternatively, you could use photocopiable page 104.

What to do

In contrast to the 'Ideas book' (see page 27), this log is intended specifically for recording the main learning points from your training courses and professional reading. It will give you the space to reflect on them either at the time or later.

Start the log at the first double-page spread in your notebook. Rule a margin down the left-hand edge of the left-hand page and write in the heading 'Dates'. The remaining space on that page should be headed 'Learning points' and the opposite page should be headed 'Thoughts, reactions, reflections' or something similar. A quick note of a particular point at the time can be followed at leisure with comments. For example, you may have recorded the main features of collaborative work discussed at a course on classroom organisation. Later on, you might jot down some thoughts on their implications for your class and the need for balance of class, collaborative and individual work.

These sheets can then all be stored together in a file for quick and easy reference.

Follow-up

Kept regularly, this kind of 'log' develops into an extremely valuable learning record which can be especially useful to refer to when applying for a job.

'What will I need tomorrow?'

Objective
To prepare effectively for the following day in the classroom.

What you need
Photocopiable page 105.

What to do
Spend five minutes, no more, as soon as possible after the end of each school day filling in the chart on photocopiable page 105. Use it in conjunction with your normal planning documents to prepare, however briefly, for the next day.

Knowing, in outline, what you are going to do the next day is a major time-saver and stress-reducer, as well as being very much in the interests of the children. This activity is not intended, of course, to replace your normal planning; it is really a 'focusing' technique designed to help you to think of what needs to be done in advance. Try it in other contexts, such as preparing for an important meeting or a potentially difficult discussion with a parent.

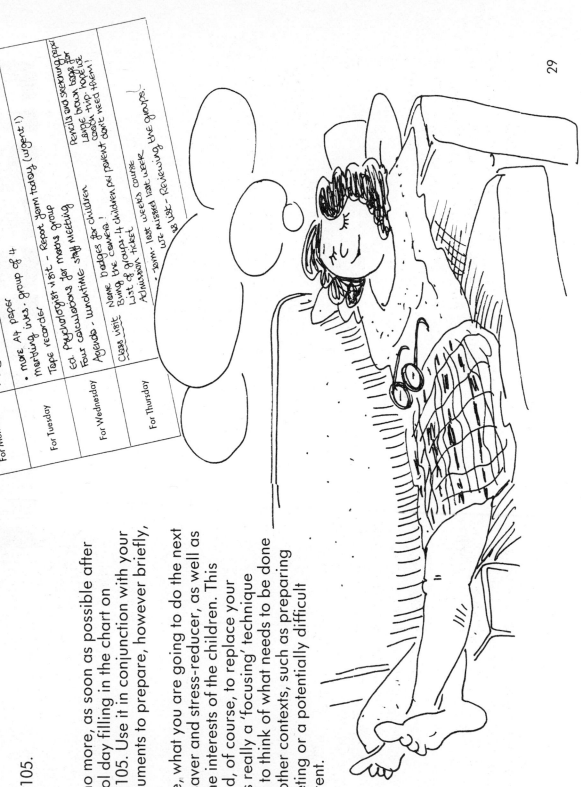

Week starting 21st May	What I need tomorrow
For Monday	• Lower School planning meeting - bring 3 children's folders • magnetism box - from science resource area this week • my turn for the computer this week
For Tuesday	• more A4 paper • marking inks - group of 4 Tape recorder
For Wednesday	Ed. Psychologist visit - Report from today (urgent!) Four calculators for maths group Agenda - lunchtime staff meeting Pencils and sketching paper Class visit: Name badges for children Bring the camera! List of groups - 4 children per parent don't need them! Large brown tape for coach trip, hope use Admission ticket
For Thursday	Form - last week's course Form - missed last week 28 List - Reviewing the groups.

In the classroom

Classroom time is probably the scarcest resource of all and should therefore be managed actively. This section deals with two main categories of time management in the classroom. First, it deals with the things that the teacher can do himself in terms of classroom administration, lesson planning and the management of children's learning. Second, it offers suggestions for helping the children to collaborate with each other and take more responsibility for the management of their own learning – both saving teacher-time and improving the quality of their own work.

Most children need opportunities to plan and think together with other children. As well as being very good educational practice, this can be a great time-saver for the class teacher. The activities in this section are designed to support collaborative group work in pairs or small groups of three or four – children are often expected to work collaboratively in groups that are much too big.

The tasks set for such groups should be genuinely collaborative; that is, the children need to co-operate in order to achieve the task. Much group work in schools involves children sitting in a group, but all working separately on individual tasks. A co-operative task may include individual contributions for instance, a group writing a newsletter might organise themselves for part of the time to write individually, but they still need to plan and work together to achieve the overall task. Encourage the children to talk among themselves, try things out and solve their own difficulties within the group. Try consciously to make them less dependent on you and to promote group responsibility for the task.

Working in this way cannot suddenly be introduced to a class. It takes much practice and support. If the class has little experience of working like this, start off in a gradual way with tasks which involve pairs.

If the children in your class are allowed to support each other's learning they will need both opportunities and encouragement to do so. Mixed-ability group work is a proven promoter of effective learning for children of all abilities. Much group work in schools, however, consists in children of similar ability sitting together but working individually, so you need tasks where the group have to work together.

Effective implementation of the following suggestions, especially those relating to greater collaboration and self-management, does depend on teachers taking regular short periods of time to reflect on what they are doing and what they want to achieve. It is important to feel that it is legitimate to reflect on good practice, as this is the best way to improve the quality of learning experiences for children.

A useful model for reflection is the learning model proposed by an American psychologist Donald Kolb (see diagram). Kolb suggests that there are four elements of learning and that all four are, in varying degrees, part of successful learning experiences. The starting point for learning could be any of them – for instance, reflective observation could be a starting point just as much as a concrete experience or active experimentation.

● Concrete experience – things that actually happen to us, planned or unplanned.
● Reflective observation – thinking about our experiences and observations and trying to learn from them.
● Abstract conceptualisation – trying to make sense of experience by attempting generalisations, looking for alternatives, trying out theories and constructing alternatives. All of us, adults and children alike, need opportunities to do this as it is a central aspect of development.

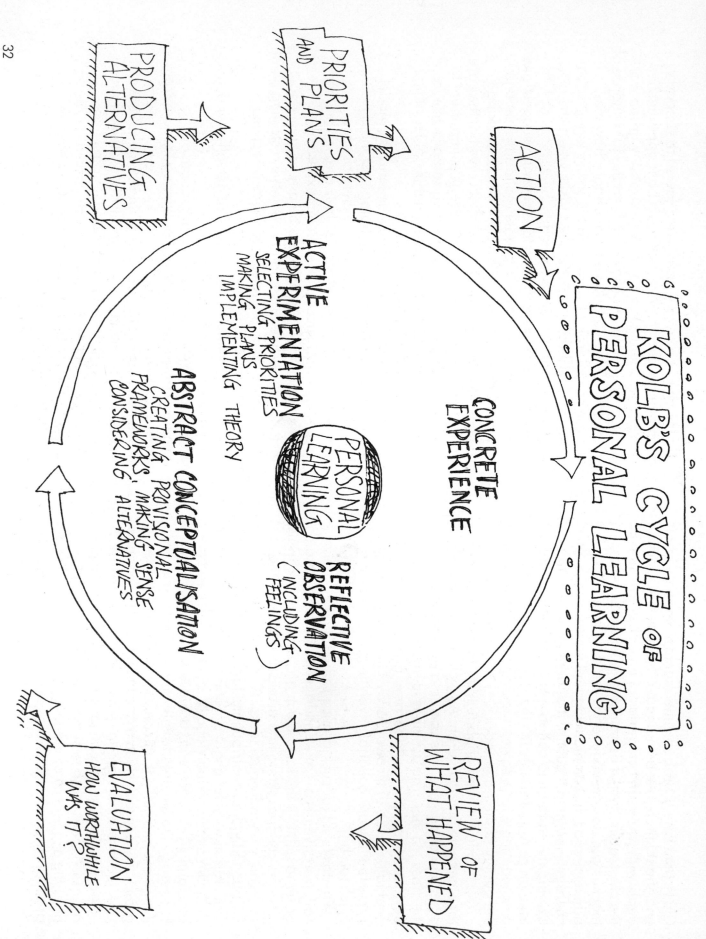

KOLB'S CYCLE OF PERSONAL LEARNING

PRODUCING ALTERNATIVES

PRIORITIES AND PLANS

ACTION

ACTIVE EXPERIMENTATION
SELECTING PRIORITIES
MAKING PLANS
IMPLEMENTING THEORY

CONCRETE EXPERIENCE

ABSTRACT CONCEPTUALISATION
CREATING PROVISIONAL
FRAMEWORKS, MAKING SENSE
CONSIDERING ALTERNATIVES

PERSONAL LEARNING

REFLECTIVE OBSERVATION
(INCLUDING FEELINGS)

EVALUATION
HOW WORTHWHILE
WAS IT?

REVIEW OF WHAT HAPPENED

Establishing any class routine

Objective

To save time by establishing key class routines.

What you need

Any carefully planned and thought-out classroom routine, for example, how the children get access to basic materials; what happens when the teacher needs to talk to the whole class and so on.

What to do

First, be clear what a routine is: it is a classroom management tool which is applied as a matter of course and should not need to be reinforced on every occasion it is applied. Classrooms where 'routines' have to be reinforced constantly are places where learning time is being wasted. Time spent reinforcing a routine initially will be recouped later when it becomes a habit. Therefore, a major initial effort to establish key routines is essential, but do not try to institute more than one or

There is more than one place to start – in fact, it is possible to start anywhere. The model does suggest, however, that if a stage is left out, then the learning will not be as effective as it could be, for example, if you always go from concrete experience to active experimentation, leaving out the reflective stage.

● Active experimentation – doing things in the real world, seeing what works, making and implementing plans.

It would be fair to say that as a profession we are good at providing children with opportunities for valuable experiences and for active experimentation, but perhaps we might give more attention to the two reflective elements, both for ourselves and for the children we teach. It seems to be the experience of teachers that learning is both more effective and quicker if we do so. For instance, teachers are sometimes disappointed that an exciting experience provided for the children does not have immediate results in the work they produce: the reason is that children need time to assimilate, think about, experiment with and accommodate to new experiences.

The model is also valuable in understanding how a school can learn and develop. One cannot expect to leap from experience to action and expect to achieve something lasting if the reflection and assimilation stages are left out.

two new routines at once, and not too many in total. There is a danger that a class can become routine-bound, with procedures for so many things that individual initiative is stifled.

Follow-up

All classroom routines should be the subject of regular review. The wise teacher will also seek feedback about classroom routines from her class and will ensure that the children are aware of the reasons for them. This is not, of course, to say that children always have to see the reason for a routine in order to apply it, but it is a part of education to develop an understanding of the need for some rules.

A routine for starting the day

Objective

To start the day in an organised and time-effective way which sets a climate for learning.

What you need

A plan for starting the day which ensures that the children settle at productive learning activities immediately they arrive in the classroom and which enables you to dispatch efficiently any essential administrative routines.

What to do

Few things create a more favourable impression, especially to parents, than a class of children coming into their room and purposefully getting down to some

learning activity without the apparent intervention of their teacher. The tone for the day is set and time is used productively right from the start.

The first element needed to implement such a plan is to dispel uncertainty. The children must know what they have to do before they come in to the classroom in the morning and you should not have to tell them every time. To give you time to take the register and deal with other essential business, the children need to understand that you cannot be disturbed. What they do, therefore, has to be:

● something they know about in advance;
● something that can be done without you;
● something silent – to speed up register and money routines.

Here are some suggestions for possible activities:

● silent reading;
● handwriting practice;

- making a fair copy of a piece of work;
- completing a self-assessment or evaluation sheet (for older children).

Post the list of approved activities where the children can see it – emphasise that no one is to approach you during this time except in emergency. If they do, smile and point silently to the list. Draw their attention to the list before home time; encourage the children to choose in advance for the next day if they can and to balance their choices across the week.

Time spent by the teacher in getting the start of the day right is well spent and will lead to much time being saved.

A 'going home' routine

Objective

To establish and reinforce effectively a routine for the end of the day.

What you need

A clear and easily understood plan.

What to do

Time needs to be managed carefully towards the end of a school day so that the children leave behind a tidy classroom, in a calm and orderly manner, with all their possessions and with anything else they need to take home.

Do not leave it until the last minute to clear up and collect the coats – the most organised class needs time to do this job properly. Do bring your class together to bid them farewell and to check up on all of them. Chaos and tears at the end of a day are very destructive of teacher morale – in contrast, children departing quietly and calmly make you feel all the more ready to prepare for next day.

Here are some tips for organising an effective and enjoyable going-home routine:

● Give a clear message that it is now time to tidy up. Each child should be responsible for tidying up his or her own work, but there should also be group tidy-up tasks.

● Tell the children where to go when they have finished – back to their seats, to the carpet area and so on.

● Bring the whole class together towards the end of the day. Allow about five minutes for story telling, reading a short poem, a quiz or an anecdote.

● Ensure that the children leave in an orderly manner. Younger children enjoy fun ways of being identified as ready to leave – for example, all those wearing white socks or those with door number less than 10. With older children, it is better to identify groups in order of readiness.

● Do not make it a race to get ready; emphasise that the children have to tidy up properly and behave well while they are getting ready to go home.

Decide exactly what routine you want to follow and write it down. This will be helpful to anybody else who may have to take your class. Tell your children what you want and then be prepared to practise it intensively to start with.

Follow-up

Write down your class routines and inform your colleagues that you would like them to maintain them with your class while you are away. This way, you will ensure that the time you have spent training the children will not be wasted.

Establishing a code of conduct

Objective

To agree and implement a minimum set of rules for the children.

What you need

Discussion and planning time with your class – which will save much time later.

What to do

Inform the children that together you are going to agree a simple set of class rules which everyone will then have to follow. Start off by gathering as many ideas as possible, including your own. A school behaviour policy is very helpful at this stage. Discuss each suggestion with the children, emphasising reasons and justifications. It is very important that you do not cut this stage short. The intention is that a final list of perhaps six to eight rules should emerge. It is important to make each as clear and brief as possible, for example, 'We

do not talk when our teacher asks us to listen' or 'We all have to take care of our classroom and the things in it'.

Make a large poster of the class rules and display it prominently in the classroom. Draw attention to it on appropriate occasions. The children could also make their own rule cards to keep in desks or trays.

Follow-up

● Try out the agreed rules for two or three weeks – this is a crucial period, when infringements must be pointed out clearly and emphasis placed on individual responsibility to apply collectively agreed rules. Afterwards, review the rules with the children and make appropriate changes.
● Inform parents and carers about the code of conduct and give them a copy of it.

Planning the classroom layout

Objective

To involve the children in decisions about effective use of classroom space.

What you need

Two or three copies of the photocopiable grid of squared paper on page 106.

What to do

It is very worthwhile to involve your children in planning the classroom layout – their ideas may save you hours of thinking time. Think of the children as users of the classroom space with considerable practical experience of what it is like to work in it! Ask them to think about such matters as:

● access to materials;
● individual storage space;
● pathways through the classroom;
● displaying their work to best advantage;
● wet area;
● quiet area.

Draw the outline of your classroom shape on the grid provided on photocopiable page 106. Cut out to scale from another copy of the grid as many tables as you have in your classroom. Try out various arrangements of these tables on the classroom grid sheet. This saves a lot of time moving the furniture and is especially helpful in visualising the various access pathways through the class, for example, to the library or painting area. Cut out scale shapes of other classroom furniture and add them as necessary. A tiny blob of Blu-Tack or similar under each shape will keep them in place temporarily on the grid.

Follow-up

Ask the children to gather evidence of how they use the classroom over a period of time. This should include observation and questionnaires. Well-presented evidence is a powerful argument in competing for extra resources.

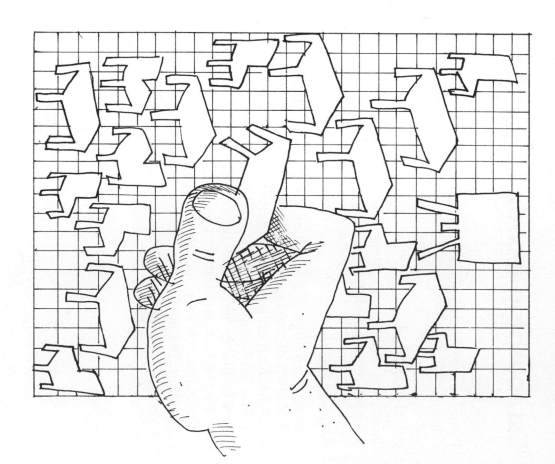

A place for small equipment

Objective
To save time by ensuring prompt return of small equipment.

What you need
A piece of thick sugar paper, cut to fit the table or surface top where the equipment will be stored, clear self-adhesive plastic, a felt-tipped pen.

What to do
Checking that various items of small equipment used during an activity have all been put back in place and then working out exactly what is missing can be quite time-consuming. One way to speed up this process is to outline on sugar paper each piece of equipment to be placed on it. Label each outline inside the shape and cover the whole sheet with plastic film. You can then attach it to the table-top or surface where the equipment is to be kept. It makes it much quicker and easier to establish where the items should go and just what is missing.

Follow-up
This suggestion is particularly useful if used with your personal collection of equipment, books or other items brought in for the children to look at or use.

Devolving responsibility

Objective

To develop children's capacity to take responsibility for aspects of classroom life.

What to do

All children should have some clearly defined responsibilities for classroom maintenance. It is, after all, their daily working environment. Older children might organise themselves into groups with specific responsibilities; younger children will need more guidance. The groups should be no bigger than four and it is important that they have a mix of boys and girls. All the children in the class should be organised into groups but it is important not to abandon the concept of individual responsibility for general maintenance and tidying up.

In a class of 30 or so children, you could have eight groups with responsibilities rotating on a monthly or half-termly basis. Here are some possible 'job descriptions':

● Class library/book corner – checking condition of books, making a repairs list, helping display the books attractively, choosing and displaying a 'Book of the Week', mounting and displaying book reviews;
● Stationery/exercise books – maintaining paper stocks in the trays, tidying exercise-book piles;
● Art area – general maintenance, tidying equipment;
● Registers/dinner money – delivering/collecting the registers (but not register-taking), counting and totalling amounts.
● Urgent messages – delivering these (but only urgent ones, otherwise other people's time is wasted).

● Displays – maintenance, assisting with repairs/helping to mount new displays.
● Wet playtime – giving out and collecting wet-play games and equipment.
● Class pets – duties related to their feeding, cleaning and exercise. Also taking pets home for holidays if parents agree.

At the end of their term of office, reward each group with a certificate of merit. You could also award a special certificate for high achievement to those groups who have really earned it.

Follow-up

Try to instil in the children a sense of responsibility, individual and collective, for their environment, including the school grounds. It requires some time and effort to establish the necessary routines, but it saves time in the long run, as well as contributing to the children's education.

Teaching pairs

Objective
To involve children in supporting the learning of others through the teaching of a clearly identified skill.

What you need
A specific skill you want to develop in all the children.

What to do
There are many classroom routines and skills which both help the children in their tasks and save the teacher a great deal of time. Familiarity with school- and classroom equipment, library skills, mounting skills and good knowledge of the school layout are just some of them.

Identify a specific skill that the children have already spent some time mastering. Make sure that a fair number are familiar with the initial stages of acquiring this skill. Form one or two pairs of children, each pair containing one child who is fairly competent at the skill and one who is less so. These groups will have the responsibility for introducing the skill to somebody new to the class or at the very earliest stage of reinforcing the skill. The less competent child in the group will gain by further practising the skill through having to show others, while the more competent one will often find other and better ways of performing the task; but both children in the pair will have the satisfaction of teaching somebody else.

Ideally, every child in the class should be in at least one teaching pair. There should also be teaching pairs across a range of skills and knowledge. Whatever time and trouble it takes initially to set up the teaching pairs, you will find it a great time-saver, as well as a means of promoting collaborative learning.

A record of pupils' preferred learning styles

Objective
To record and have easy access to information concerning how children learn best.

What you need
Photocopiable page 107.

Preferred learning styles

Class: 4a

Date	Name of child	Preferred style(s) – examples/evidence
4/3/92	Claire Jones	Enjoys working in a pair – eg. book she made with Nisha from Reception. getting more confident in a larger group.
9/3/92	George Attfield	Confident articulate in most learning situations. Has enjoyed learning to support others less able and confident.
9/3/92	Margaret Fraser	Very able. prefers to work alone, or in a pair with a friend. Working with the bridge making group helped her to be less impatient.

What to do
Children vary in their preferences for learning styles. A record of their preferred learning styles can be an effective time-saver. Try to keep your chart as simple as you can if you are not using photocopiable page 107, but avoid 'pigeon-holing' your children. Review the record regularly. Use the record to:

- help you to organise groups;
- provide valuable information for other teachers;
- obtain assessment information for a variety of purposes, including the National Curriculum.

Queues at your desk

Objective
To reduce time-wasting queues at your desk.

What you need
No specific requirements.

What to do
Long queues are a major time waster and although a proper cure involves looking at your whole approach to classroom management, it is worth dealing with the symptoms immediately. Insist that only two children are at your desk at any one time, one talking to you and one waiting. This may cause some problems initially, but it is essential to do something about the queues before they become a way of life and a classic time-wasting activity for some children, comparable to an extended visit to the toilet!

Here are some suggestions for preventing long queues:
• Tell the children in advance about your plan for the day.
• Have the day's tasks clearly displayed somewhere in the classroom so that the children know what to do next.
• Allow the children to help one another where appropriate, especially with spelling. This is different from copying!
• Allow the children some freedom in organising how and in what order they do their work.
• Look carefully at the length and depth of the learning activities – are there too many ten-minute fillers?

• Suggest ongoing tasks the children can return to when they have completed the set work. This could be completing a book cover or a piece of embroidery, mounting work or filling in a self-examination sheet.

Desk queues are a symptom that all is not well with classroom organisation. If you seem to be suffering from this symptom you might look at your practice in relation to whole-class teaching. For example, what provision do you make for slower- and faster-than-average learners? Perhaps the key question is, 'Do the children know what to do next?'

Using a video recorder effectively

Objective
To save time and unnecessary disruption by choosing appropriate times for your class to watch television programmes.

What you need
A video recorder (remember that you do not need a television set to record programmes, only to play them back), photocopiable page 108.

What to do
If at all possible, record all the educational television programmes your class watches. Some schools have a video connected to an aerial in a secure store, which automatically records all the week's programmes. Do not watch programmes at the time of their broadcast unless you have a specific educational reason for doing so. Quite apart from the necessity for the teacher to have a preview of the learning opportunities for the class, watching a recording is definitely a time-saver.

How often does a class, disrupted by the need to adhere to a fixed schedule, end up watching some of the previous programme or missing the start? Both are instances of poor time management and are disruptive to learning.

Use photocopiable page 108 to note times and channels of all the programmes you would like to record. Ideally, one member of the support staff should be responsible for recording but even if you end up doing it yourself, you will find that a handy list of all the programmes you want to record is a definitive time-saver.

The same points apply to radio programmes.

Follow-up
If you have access to a video camera, try using the following ways to help you organise the day.
● Make a video of yourself giving instructions, briefing an activity for group work.
● Film yourself reading a short story and use it in read-along sessions.
● Film a group of children explaining how they went about a task. Use the tape to brief subsequent groups.

Marking work in class

Objective

To save time by marking some work in class with the child, as opposed to taking all work home.

What you need

No specific requirements.

What to do

The traditional way to mark children's work is to let them bring it to you on completion. However, this often leads to queues of children doing nothing and standing waiting. A better way to mark work in class is to let the class know that you will be marking work for the next half hour and call children to you individually. Another possibility is to sit at a table with a small group of children and mark their work individually while raising

particular learning points with the whole class – this works best when the individuals have been working on a similar task. If a group of children have been working on a collaborative task, the outcomes should always be 'marked' with the group as a whole, not with the children individually.

There are of course occasions in a primary classroom, particularly with older children, where work requires more detailed written comment, when a teacher needs to collect up the books and mark them all together outside class time. However, marking work with the child present is good practice as well as being time-efficient and specific planning for this is time well spent. The assessment requirements of the National Curriculum are also a spur to this kind of marking because they necessitate assessment of *individual* levels of attainment. This can be done more efficiently and reliably in conjunction with the child.

'Formative' marking

Objective

To use the time spent marking individual children's work in the classroom in a way which promotes learning and uses teacher-time effectively.

What you need

No specific requirements.

What to do

Most teachers find that marking at least some of the children's work in the classroom is valuable in terms of discussion with the individual child. The opportunity should always be taken when marking in class to guide the child sensitively towards the next learning activity, whether connected with the work being marked or not. Some teachers do this instinctively, but most of us need actively to practise this important professional skill. Any such marking session should end with the question 'What next?'

For example, you have just marked a child's work on the design of a medieval castle. This could lead to an assignment in design and technology such as making a working portcullis or to a shared story-writing project from which it may become clear that the child has little knowledge of the Middle Ages as an historical period and that some basic revision might be in order.

The active teacher

Objective

To increase the 'learning' contact you have with individuals and groups in your class.

What you need

No specific requirements.

What to do

However you organise your class and whatever the learning and teaching styles you want to promote, it is a considerable waste of your time to be sitting at your desk, especially doing routine tasks, while the children are working. This is prime time to interact with the children and support their learning in all sorts of ways. Working with a group, discussions with individuals and unobtrusive dealing with disruptions can be undertaken more effectively by the teacher who gets about!

Do you think they would have had a 'magic eye' in those days, Thomas?

Try to focus your interventions on the children's work rather than the 'management' and control issues which are often the staple diet of classroom interaction between the teacher and child. Research (for example, the ILEA *School Matters*) has shown clearly that talking to pupils about their work promotes achievement, while management talk, especially about classroom routines, does not.

Planning entitlement activities in topic work

Objective

To make sure that every child experiences a 'core' set of learning activities within every class topic.

What you need

A class topic.

What to do

A lot of topic work that is carried out in classrooms makes very poor use of valuable learning time. One reason for this is that teachers do not always decide what learning activities within the topic are going to be experienced by *all* the children in the class and plan appropriately for this 'core' entitlement. Therefore, it is worth planning and resourcing carefully a set of perhaps six or seven substantial learning activities, certainly no more, that would be included in the topic work. These learning activities would then be experienced by all the children in the class. For

example, all the children in the class would be asked to record weather conditions for a week, while working on their half-term topic of the weather.

Follow-up

Once the core activities have been planned and delivered, the teacher can afford to encourage some development of further individual and group interests within the topic. The big time-saving is that only these entitlement activities need to be carefully planned in advance – there is no need to over-prepare. Teachers in well-established collaborative planning groups might also explore the possibility of sharing the planning, resourcing and even delivery of these learning activities. Involvement of all staff in cross-curricular planning ensures worthwhile content and avoids repetition of material by year groups.

Topic work record sheet

Objective

To keep a central and easily accessible record of topic work completed over the year.

What you need

Photocopiable page 109.

What to do

Photocopiable page 109 should be completed termly. Use it to record such things as the areas of the National

Topic work record sheet	Class 6 P	Year 6
Autumn	Topic title Tudors Hist/Language	
	Comments – reaction of children, National Curriculum delivery, N. Curriculum coverage. Much stimulating Art and Language work. We got onto Tudor sailors and their voyages, so we did quite a lot of geography.	
	Topic title Theatres Drama/Art/Hist/Music	
	Comments – Much enjoyed by the pupils – good link with Tudors. Made our Christmas production a real learning experience. Lots of N.C. work covered.	
Spring	Topic title Rain forests Science/Geog	
	Comments – Ecological focus enjoyed by pupils – a lot of geography done. Science content less promising than it worked initially. Children most interested in conservation aspect	
	Topic title Timetables Maths/Lang	
	Comments – Excellent, focused topic – great deal of Maths covered. The children brought in lots of timetables. Planning round-the-world journeys great fun	

Curriculum covered when working on a particular topic, the learning outcomes of each topic and the reaction of the children to each topic.

At the end of the year hand over the completed sheets to the next teacher who will then be able to see almost at a glance the areas already covered. This valuable information will help him plan for future topics, avoid repetition and build on skills which have already been mastered.

Same activity – different outcomes

Objective

To plan activities which are appropriate for children of all abilities.

What you need

A class topic.

What to do

If we wish to ensure that a set of planned learning activities within a class topic are suitable for all the children in a class, the activities clearly have to be suitable for all abilities. The basic learning experience will be the same, but it will be necessary to allow for different outcomes. The question you will have to ask yourself is whether children at both ends of the ability spectrum can undertake this activity and achieve different outcomes, appropriate to their ability. For example, within a topic on journeys, you might decide that one substantial learning experience would be to visit a bus station and that the task would be to write an account of the visit.

At one end of the ability spectrum, the outcome might be a simple account of the visit and some sketches; in relation to that particular child, the achievement might well be considerable. At the other end, a child might produce a variety of highly accomplished writing, both factual and imaginative.

Follow-up

In consultation with other teachers, prepare a list of learning activities suitable for mixed-ability groups.

The planning cycle – clarify, plan, do, review

Objective

To help children understand and operate a planning cycle.

What you need

Small groups (pairs, initially) working together on a collaborative task.

What to do

Clarify: although there may be some overlap with the next stage, clarification of the task is an important process which needs separate identification. It is important for everyone in the group to be clear about the task itself and children need practice with this. Introduce the task and ask the children to talk to each other briefly about what they think they will have to do.

Emphasise that everybody in the group needs to understand the task and that the group members need to help each other in getting that understanding. Do not be tempted to give more and more detailed explanations in response to queries; give the children time to talk it over and to clarify it themselves. After a while, ask the children to state what the task is. You will often be pleasantly surprised!

Another possible starting point is a suggestion from the children about what they would like to do. Children quite often come to their teachers with a request to do something in particular – if they have had some training and experience in task clarification, you can expect them to come with a clear and thought-out statement of what they want to do rather than breathless incoherence!

Plan: once the children are clear about the task, the next step is to plan it. Again the temptation is to give them a ready-made plan, especially if there is any hesitation or uncertainty. What the children need to know is that they have the responsibility to plan, but that their teacher will support them if they get in a tangle. A framework to get them started is usually necessary and one method is to provide a list of written questions.
● What are you hoping to end up with? (For example, collage, a model, a newsletter page.)
● What needs to be done to achieve it?
● What materials and tools will you need?
● Who will do what?

There is no need to insist on a written plan – indeed this may affect adversely the children's motivation and is not usually recommended. What the group needs is to be clear among themselves how they are going to approach the task and to explain to the teacher how they have agreed to do the task. Initially the teacher will want to hear this before the group start work, but as everybody gets more confident, the group can go on to the next stage without consulting the teacher, who can then monitor the plans selectively.

Do: working collaboratively from an agreed plan to the completion of the task. If the children understand the task and have a clear plan, they will want to get on and do it. Well-timed interventions which support their learning are, of course, valuable, but unnecessary ones, especially when things are going well, are a waste of time for the children and the teacher. Worst of all, this may lead the children to think you are not really serious about giving them some responsibility for their own learning. Teachers need to value both the process and the outcome, referring back to the plan the children made and the discussions they had about clarifying the task, as well as commenting on what the children have actually done.

Review: how did we do? When the task is completed or when the time is up, there should be a review which looks not only at the end product (the outcome) but also at the planning and its effectiveness (the process). Review is not a complicated process. Explain to the children that they are going to look back at everything they have done, the task clarification, the planning and the actual work done. Use the following three questions as a framework.

● What went well?
● What didn't go so well?
● What will we do differently next time?

Initially the children will probably concentrate on the actual outcome – their 'work'. It is important for the teacher to widen the discussion to include the whole process, to reinforce the learning point that the quality of the planning process has a great effect on the quality of the outcome. When the children have had sufficient practice, they should be able to hold their own reviews and report back to the teacher, either verbally or in writing.

A review process has little purpose unless the children are able to work collaboratively on a fairly regular basis – the learning from review is cumulative, with new knowledge being applied the next time. There is substantial initial teacher input but the time saving really becomes apparent when the children become more confident and independent learners.

Review

What went well?
What didn't go well?
What will we do
differently next time?

An overview of the planning cycle

Objective
To give an overview of the whole process as outlined in the previous activity.

What you need
Photocopiable page 110.

What to do
Photocopiable page 110 conveniently collects together the whole of the suggested process of 'clarify, plan, do, review'. The children would only use it by themselves after they have had experience of the four individual stages and have a feel for the whole process.

The process is a cycle, not a one-off event. Teachers who wish to try it do need to provide a careful teaching programme initially before the children can operate it by themselves, but the potential rewards in terms of effective learning and the saving of teacher time are considerable.

the planning cycle

1. The task

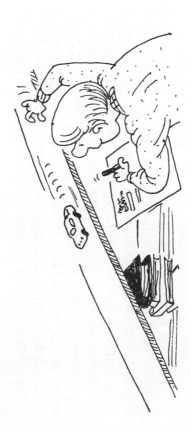

Teaching notes
Although the planning process focuses on collaborative group work, it is quite possible to teach the various stages of the process formally through class lesson and discussion – there is no need to explain the process to every individual group. However, the real educational value and time-saving benefits only become apparent when children can operate it themselves and this takes practice. A common mistake, especially with children who have little experience of collaborative group work, is to make the groups too big – for younger children, pairs or at most, groups of three are big enough, while even for older children groups of six are really too large.

It is also worth remembering that while the task itself should be a collaborative one, the recording and writing up does not. A group of three might build a wheeled vehicle and collect experimental data together on how far it would travel from the top of an incline, but there might well be separate accounts written up about what happened and what conclusions were drawn. Teachers may not be able to observe the group at work in any detail but they can assess individual learning through such accounts and through discussions with individual children.

Self-evaluation in the classroom

Objective

To increase children's active involvement in their own learning through reflection on what they do.

What you need

Photocopiable page 111.

What to do

Each child should have his or her own copy of the self-evaluation sheet on photocopiable page 111. This could be stored in a central file and each child could keep a copy of it in a work file or, best of all, with their profile/record of achievement if they have one.

Ask the children at the conclusion of a substantial activity to fill it in for that activity (do not trivialise this by asking them to do this after every single thing they do).

Children who have worked collaboratively should be encouraged to discuss their thoughts with the others involved. Older children should be able to fill their own sheets. Younger ones will need help which, however time-consuming for the teacher, will provide valuable information about their learning. It is very important to concentrate on the individual learning and achievement rather than bring in a competitive element which will only encourage the children to be less than honest.

You can use children's self-evaluation records in a number of ways. First, you can positively reinforce the child's achievements – building on success is a key element in effective learning. Second, you can use the sheet as a basis for a sensitive discussion of things which did not go so well. Third, you can help the child be more explicit – for example, ask what exactly he meant by having learned 'lots of things about the Normans'. And, finally, you could start a discussion of the next related learning task with the information from the 'What I need to do next' section.

Group work evaluation sheet

Objective
To increase the active involvement of children in their own learning, through reflection on what they do.

What you need
Photocopiable page 112.

What to do
Photocopiable page 112 is intended to be used by older children collectively. Ask a group of children who have worked together on a substantial activity to complete a copy of the form collaboratively. They can nominate a scribe or complete a part of the form each. However, it is vital that they discuss their thoughts with others in the group and represent the opinions of the group as a whole.

This process of group self-evaluation provides valuable information for both the teacher and the children, which can be used in the following ways:
- in assessment, including National Curriculum assessment;
- to help the children do better next time;
- as part of individual profile or record of achievement;
- as an agenda to discuss with the group;
- as information for parents.

Group work evaluation sheet

Names *Julie Gary + Peter*

What did you do together?

We designed and made a model made from only paper which spanned 50cm and supported a model car without collapsing. We worked together to plan how we were going to do it. We made a bridge. We did all the testing together. We all had ideas which...out

What did you do separately?

Julie and Gary made one test model together. Peter made one test model by himself. Gary did a lot of the cutting, when we decided which one was best. Each of us made notes in our work-books. Julie did a lot of the paper shaping.

What were you pleased about in your work?

We actually made the bridge and it worked. We worked well together without arguing much. Nobody felt left out. We learned about what makes a bridge strong and how strong a paper bridge can be.

What were you not so pleased about?

We were a bit impatient and didn't think enough before we did something, so we took longer to do it.

Children's learning log

Objective
To save teacher time and to increase pupil motivation and achievement through appropriate involvement in record-keeping.

What you need
Photocopiable page 113.

What to do
It is a great time-saver if children become involved in their own record-keeping. Some methods of doing this, such as a record of achievement, are best considered in the context of whole-school agreements, but this activity is suitable for the individual teacher to try.

Give each child a copy of photocopiable page 113. Explain to them what it is for and suggest ways of filling it in. Ask the children to complete the sheet every week, preferably working in pairs. Both children can talk to each other about what they have done and then compile their own lists.

Thinking about what they have learned is a major step forward for many children and it should not be rushed: some children need to stay at the 'Main things I did' stage for a while. The question 'What can I do now that I could not do before?' may be helpful.

The children should be able to see a purpose in doing this – this purpose should relate to the notice their teacher takes of their comments and the action which might follow. In the example, it would be important to take note of the suggestions made, even though it would be unlikely if all of them could be followed. The teacher could read through a whole set of these sheets in 15–20 minutes and obtain a valuable context for planning next week's activities, as well as having a ready-made piece of individual record-keeping.

This activity has to become a part of classroom routine for its full benefits to be realised – it could be modified to be done fortnightly with older children. The emphasis is on looking back over a whole week or fortnight.

Follow-up

Try not to get involved in doing this for the children. Instead encourage them to get help from each other. This, together with the self-evaluation form (see page 111), will provide valuable information directly from the children about themselves and their learning which can be used in all sorts of different ways; for example, for National Curriculum assessment, identifying difficulties and weaknesses, as a focus for discussion with parents and so on.

The learning partnership

The management of other adults, both in the classroom and increasingly outside it, has become a significant part of the class teacher's role. This section contains activities related to two particular aspects of this management; extra classroom help of various kinds and the running of efficient meetings.

Meetings are an important feature of teachers' professional lives – even quite new teachers find themselves having to organise and even chair them. Badly organised meetings can waste an enormous amount of time and divert energy away from the classroom, but good ones are very motivating. It is therefore important for teachers to understand what a good meeting should be like, not only because they might need to run them, but also so that they can be sensitive, constructive participants.

The potential of extra classroom help for both enhancing children's learning and making more time for the class teacher is considerable – but some time has to be invested initially in planning for their participation if real benefits are to ensue.

Analysis of part-time teacher help

Objective
To clarify the current situation in your classroom in respect of part-time teacher help and any changes which you would like to be made.

What you need
Photocopiable page 114.

What to do
Use photocopiable page 114 to record the current situation regarding extra teaching help in your class and what you would actually like the situation to be. Record the reasons you have for your preferred situation.

Part-time teacher help analysis

The present situation in my class

Current help   Mrs Shaw

How is it used?   5 mornings a week

How effective is it?   Good with children generally. Enables me to delegate some tasks and get on with more pressing things.

My preferred situation

What help do I really need?   Full time classroom assistant or 2 job sharing - one morning one afternoon

How should this be related to children's learning needs?   Assistant can supervise activities set by me while I concentrate on slower learners

How will we plan/liaise together?   Arrange a weekly meeting to sort out priorities

Reasons for my preferred situation

Do t

Follow-up
Once you are clear about the present situation and what you actually want, you are in a much better position to discuss any changes. Many school situations stay the same not so much because there is active opposition to doing something different, but because nobody has actually thought out what they want and why. Clear analysis and action at this stage will save time later.

Summary of extra help (teaching and support)

Objective

To provide a permanent and easily available record of extra teaching and support staff in a classroom for all the teachers involved.

What you need

Photocopiable page 115.

What to do

Once extra teaching and support staff have been allocated, spend some time discussing with the people concerned what it is they will be doing, and when they will be doing it. When you have agreed both the timing

Class	Person and time	Summary of agreed tasks/planning
Mon	Mrs Rashid 11·00–12:30	Mrs Rashid will support a small group of 4 regularly within class - (writing accounts of their class visit this week)
Tues		
Wed	Miss Harvey 1·30–2·00	Whole class - Singing & Percussion work - will tie in with the topic where possible.
Thurs	9·00– 10·30 Mr Eames	My curric co-ord release time. Mr Eames (Geography specialist) will teach Map skills-he will keep records of the children's progress
Fri	11·00– 12·00 Mrs Bownes	Class exchange with Mrs Bownes - my colleague in Year ? Individually planned science activities.

and the planning of extra help, complete the grid on page 115 and confirm the accuracy of your summary with the people concerned. Once this has been done, a good deal of confusion and time will be saved, especially for newcomers to the class such as a supply teacher or a new helper.

Any clarifications, changes or disputes should be discussed with reference to this document. It provides an immediate focus for any discussion and reminds everybody concerned of what the current situation should be.

Activity information sheet

Objective

To convey accurate information, guidance and instructions to parents, or any extra helper, involved in supervising a learning activity in the classroom.

What you need

Photocopiable page 116.

What to do

Complete an activity briefing sheet for the task you are asking the parent(s) or extra helper(s) to undertake and give a copy to them. These sheets save time in both briefing the helpers and in debriefing them afterwards. They are especially useful when a parent or other helper is working with a group of children. They react extremely positively to this support as the sheet often removes a lot of their uncertainty about what to do.

Written comments on the activity can be added by the parent/helper and these can also provide valuable information about children's learning. The teacher can analyse those at leisure.

Follow-up
Discuss the form with the parents/helpers once the activity has been completed.

Donated-time register

Objective
To create a record of available classroom help.

What you need
A booklet or folder (you may find a poster more useful), a computer database, photocopiable page 117.

What to do
Donated time is time which has been offered free of charge to the school or class by individuals outside the school, on either regular or 'on-demand' basis. Your register of donated time should expand very quickly, especially if you actively seek out such help.

If you are keen to welcome parents and others into your classroom to support the children's learning, you will quite quickly gather a lot of information about who is available to help, what their skills are and what time they have available. It will save a lot of time to gather this information in one place. You will need to know how to contact the person, the skills offered and the time(s) he or she is available.

This information is ideally suited to a computer database (if not available you may find photocopiable page 117 helpful). It would enable you to retrieve such information as 'Who is available at 10am on Monday' or 'Who can help out with design and technology'. Be careful not to include information of a confidential nature, especially opinions or personal comments.

Follow-up
It might be possible to build up a class record of this kind into a school donated-time register which would be a great time-saver and a valuable resource for the school. (Ensure that you have obtained permission from individuals for inclusion in this register.)

A briefing sheet

Objective
To provide guidelines and information for adult visitors and classroom helpers.

What you need
No special requirements.

What to do
Much difficulty can be caused by adult visitors and classroom helpers who are unaware of school rules or who do not know what is appropriate professional behaviour towards children. To avoid constant individual briefings it is useful to provide a briefing sheet which can be given to each helper and visitor. This

sheet should include clear information about such matters as what to do if a child misbehaves, the need to work under teacher guidance, basic safety issues and so on. It could also explain such matters as smoking policy, where the toilets are and where to get a cup of tea. There should certainly be a clear statement about the confidentiality of information discovered while in the school, especially about individual children.

Follow-up
Develop the briefing sheet into a series of short information documents entitled, for instance, 'Talking to children' or 'Safety in the classroom'. Invite comments on the usefulness of the sheets from the visitors and helpers. Revise the sheets as necessary.

Parent conferencing

Objective
To collect and record parents' information relevant to their children's learning.

What you need
A clear framework for the information you want to collect, for example the ILEA Primary Language Record and Learning Record or your own school's record-keeping.

What to do
Parent conferencing is an idea developed initially by the ILEA's Centre for Language in Primary Education. It involves the systematic collection of information from

parents about aspects of their child's learning as shown at home. For example, in the area of language this would include experience/enjoyment of books and stories, information about speaking and listening skills and languages spoken at home. It does require an investment of time, but the outcomes in terms of knowledge about children's achievement are very productive and can help satisfy National Curriculum assessment requirements.

Some schools have used directed time for such parent interviews, which makes it possible to organise them outside class hours. Another possibility is to incorporate the idea into parents' evenings, so that they become more of a two-way process.

Follow-up

Parent conferencing need not be confined just to language, but is appropriate to other curriculum areas, as well as to obtaining information about how a particular child learns best.

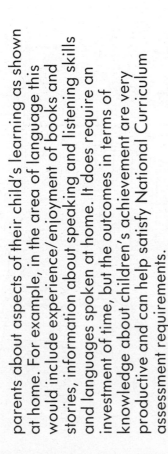

61

Parents' evening record sheet

Objective
To help you to structure your conversations with parents at parents' evenings and to keep a record of points raised.

What you need
Photocopiable page 118.

What to do
When talking to parents about their children, it is quite easy to be side-tracked by less relevant issues and, given the limited time available at a parents' evening, this can leave you short of time to discuss the points that you initially intended to raise. Photocopiable sheet 118 can therefore serve both as an aide-mémoire and as a record of parents' responses and the points they raised.

Set aside time to fill in points to be raised with parents during the evening. Six sheets will provide a complete record for a class of thirty.

Parents' evening record sheet

Class 3b Date 17 June

Appt Time	Name of child	Points to raise with parent(s)/carer(s)	Points raised by parent(s)/carer(s)
6.10	Ewart Williams	Great improvement recently in his work-really making use of considerable abilities. Talk to parents about maintaining this.	Parents confirm - say he is much more settled at home too, as he has adjusted to new baby brother. Could I keep encouraging him as he responds well to praise?
		Could parents try to	Yes they will. I have

"Make sure we speak to his English teacher..."

"GON TO DARREN2"

Most parents want to talk about their children at length. You will need to explain beforehand how much time is allotted to each child. Ask parents to prepare their points ahead of the meeting, too. If parents see that you are making a genuine effort to keep to timetable, they will be more inclined to do likewise.

A class newsletter for parents

Objective
To inform and involve parents more effectively.

What you need
Photocopiable page 119.

What to do
Twice a term, at the beginning and at the end, complete photocopiable page 119 and distribute copies to all the parents. Sending out messages and information in this way saves a lot of time and makes parents feel more positive and better informed.

The sheet will serve as a newsletter, as well as a vehicle for requesting parental assistance. It will also be an excellent image-builder for the class. Parents who are kept well-informed about what goes on in the classroom feel more positive about their involvement with school life and therefore more inclined to help out when asked.

Follow-up
Keep a file of old issues of the newsletter and give a set to parents of new children who join the class. This will help them understand their children's new school life more quickly.

Sharing a classroom activity

Objective
To save time by collaborating over the planning and delivery of classroom activities.

What you need
A colleague with a similar class to yours or with some children in the same age group.

What to do
There is no doubt that effective collaborative planning and decision-making does promote pupil learning, particularly through the improved continuity which results. It can also be a great time-saver in all sorts of ways for the teacher if well organised and carried out with enthusiasm and commitment. Collaboration prevents duplication of effort, promotes agreed procedures for working and makes time for the class teacher to make her own distinctive contributions.

Organising and resourcing a quality learning activity is usually time-consuming. With your colleague, decide on two different learning activities you both want to have in your classroom. Organise and resource one activity each and make it available to the other. This does not imply team teaching; it is simply a way to save time while still undertaking the activity yourself in your own classroom.

If you both have different curriculum strengths and expertise, then it could be very valuable to use this specialism in designing each learning activity.

Here are some other examples of collaborative planning:
● Putting two classes together occasionally (for example, for story-reading or singing) to create non-contact time.
● Using the same documentation and record-keeping.
● Dividing up the National Curriculum Orders for detailed study.
● Joint moderation of National Curriculum assessments.

Follow-up
A further development is to deliver your learning activity in your colleague's classroom.

Communal resources

Objective
To share the storage, maintenance and use of certain equipment and material.

What you need
Other colleagues, preferably in a planning team; a joint list of materials and items of equipment you could share.

What to do
Using your list, agree a plan for storage and access to the items, and arrangements for restocking and maintenance. Once the system is established this is a really effective time-saver, but don't forget to tell the children. Each contributor should take on a specific responsibility and should feel accountable to the others for making the system work. For instance, there is no need to store heavy A3 paper in each classroom or computer materials such as floppy disks if you know

where to get them and who is responsible in the team for making them available. Other materials that could easily be shared are:
● radio cassette recorders,
● specialist art materials,
● cameras,
● reference books,
● sets of maps.
Pooling classroom resources in this way saves time all around, as everyone involved in the resource-sharing scheme knows where to find things and who is responsible for their storage and maintenance.

Follow-up
A well-run system of this kind can be extended to include the children, particularly in monitoring and replenishing stocks, subject, of course, to proper safety precautions.

Collaborative planning record sheet

Objective
To have a record of decisions reached at collaborative planning meetings.

What you need
Photocopiable page 120.

What to do
It saves a great deal of time in the long run to record the outcomes of collaborative planning meetings immediately after they have taken place. Often, although decisions are taken and the appropriate action agreed upon, no-one makes a record of them and they become forgotten. Therefore, it is tremendously helpful to record action points on photocopiable page 120. This sheet provides space to write down who has agreed to do what and by when.

When you come to your next collaborative meeting it will be much easier to check on progress and follow up with further action where necessary.

Collaborative planning meeting

Date	Present	
Agreed that . . .		Action by whom and when
We should finalise details for In-service day		Jack 14te June
Need to prepare a document outlining new school policy developments		Mary 9te June
A report. back on school bullying required – draw up a guide for parents and teachers		Stuart & Eve 17te June
Need to decide on Technology co-ordinators		Maggie 11te June

Colleagues as a resource

Objective
To utilise the skills and experience of other colleagues.

What you need
An acceptance that you cannot manage the curriculum, including the National Curriculum, in isolation.

What to do
Collaborative planning is one way to tap into the skills and experience of all teachers (see page 65). Another is actively to seek out support and advice, as well as making your own skills freely available to others. Often, however, there is no systematic identification and sharing of skills among groups of teachers, although there is an informal flow of support and advice.

The tasks teachers face are so demanding nowadays that some such formal process for this, both at whole-staff and planning group level, would seem to be vital. If you are in a planning group, set aside time for a thorough discussion of what the team members can contribute in the way of skills and interests – for that matter, it would be very worth while for the whole staff to do this. The expertise and experience available among the staff of most schools is remarkable, and a systematic discussion and recording of it is something teachers usually find to be a positive experience. The same principle applies to the children – everybody has something to offer.

The subject requirements of the National Curriculum make it urgent for schools to use relevant expertise effectively. In order to achieve this, individual areas of expertise have to be first identified and recorded. A register of staff members' skills and qualifications,

especially in particular curriculum areas, can be a great time-saver in finding out which colleague to approach. A review or audit of staff skills would provide the information necessary to create the register.

Follow-up
Try to identify appropriate out-of-school skills and interests which colleagues have as well.

Why do we need a meeting?

Objective
To clarify why a meeting is to be held and what the expected results are intended to be.

What you need
A proposal for a meeting, photocopiable page 121.

Meeting planning sheet	Date	4 May

Why have the meeting?

Purposes	What outcomes are required?
1. To agree a final version of the Learning Policy	1. Final version agreed
2. To finalise arrangements for visit by 2 Governors	2. Plan for the visit
3. To discuss venue for staff party	3. Venue agreed.

Draft agenda Keep the number of items to a minimum!

1 Learning Policy	60 mins
2 Governors visit	15 mins
3 Venue for staff party	5 mins

What to do

One of the main ways of collaboration is through meetings. Teachers are increasingly having to organise these and therefore it is important to understand the fundamentals of a good meeting.

There are few things in teaching which waste more time than a poorly organised and badly run meeting. All teachers can tell horror stories of meetings which produced nothing save confusion, anger and erosion of morale. Many class teachers are increasingly involved in the organisation and running of meetings and this activity and those following are intended to help you to do both as well as possible. The focus is on the organisation and planning of meetings on one principal theme, rather than an agenda of unconnected matters – a characteristic of the average staff meeting. Of course this sort of meeting has its place, but often the key educational issue is tacked on to the end of the meeting when time is running out.

If you are responsible for planning a meeting, always start by asking yourself what the main reason for holding it is and what specific outcomes you expect. If you are not clear about either of these key points, then consider whether the meeting should be held at all. Certainly do not hold the meeting until you have definite answers. You may find the chart on photocopiable page 121 helpful.

Follow-up

It is usually very helpful to discuss purposes and outcomes of a proposed meeting with other colleagues, especially with those whose co-operation is essential to guarantee a successful meeting – perhaps the headteacher or deputy.

Constructing the agenda

Objective

To construct an agenda which plays its part in creating a successful meeting.

What you need

A clear idea of the purpose and the intended outcome of the meeting; photocopiable page 122.

What to do

An efficient meeting should have only one principal focus and there should be as few items as possible that are unconnected with it – none, if you can manage it. For example, the focus of a meeting might be to get staff reaction to the latest draft of a policy and the intended outcome could be to record the main agreed points for subsequent incorporation into the draft. This is quite enough business for one meeting and other important matters should be left for another time.

If there have to be other items, place the main one at the beginning rather than at the end of the agenda or have it as fixed business at a nominated time. Few things are more frustrating than letting the minor items dominate a meeting.

Make sure the agenda states the start and the finish time of the meeting – people have the right to know when they can expect to get away. Also, put a time against each agenda item. This is extremely helpful not only in terms of managing the meeting, but also for helping participants to be clear about the relative importance of each item.

Give an indication on the agenda of how the major item will be dealt with. Will there be any group discussion, for instance?

Follow-up

If subsequent meetings are necessary on the same theme, indicate clearly on the agenda the links with what happened and what had been agreed last time. This 'tunes in' people to what is going to happen. For example: 'Item 3 – second whole-staff discussion – draft learning policy. Discussion of new version (which includes the changes agreed at the Oct 14th meeting).'

68

Chairing a meeting

Objective

To chair a meeting which achieves its purposes and outcomes in a way that includes everybody.

What you need

If you are responsible for the process of the meeting, you need to arrange seating and make sure that any necessary materials are available. You cannot have a good meeting slouched in an armchair, so arrange the seating appropriately round a central focus, perhaps a display board or flipchart.

What to do

As chair of a meeting you need to have a very clear idea of its objective and have the skills to achieve it. Unfortunately, nearly all the people who chair meetings do so because they are the senior person there and it is often expected that the authority figure does this job. There are few schools enlightened enough to see the job of chair as being essentially about facilitating the business of the meeting and that this can often be done perfectly well by teachers other than the head and deputy.

Whole books have been written about chairing meetings so the following suggestions attempt only to skim the surface.

● Start the meeting at the stated time and do not wait for people to drift in. State clearly what time it finishes and review the agenda, pointing out the main item.

● If somebody is late, take a moment or so to tell them what is currently happening, for example, 'John, we're on Item 2 and Carol is just telling us about what she has in mind'.

Whole-staff meeting

Date: Tuesday 14 October
Place: Small hall
Start: 3.45 pm
Finish: 5.00 pm

Main purpose

The main purpose of this meeting is to finish our discussion of the Learning Policy. Draft 2 has been circulated already.

Please bring:

1. Copy of the last action minutes
2. Copy of draft 2 of the learning policy

Agenda

1. Minutes of the last meeting	5 mins
2. Update on book week plans. Information only	10 mins
3. Main item – Learning policy discussion	**60 mins**
● Discussion in pairs	10 mins
● Discussion in planning groups	20 mins
● Whole-staff comments on main points	15 mins
● Summary and What next	15 mins

Notes

● Once the item has been dealt with, keep the meeting moving on to the next item. A very good method is to summarise any agreements at the end of each item, for example, 'On this, we've agreed that Jackie and the rest of the lower school team will take on the hall display and will complete it by . . . .' If the discussion is going nowhere, remind the meeting clearly that time is running out and decisions are necessary; far better to cut the item short even without agreement than to let the meeting fall apart.

● When you get to the main item on the agenda, state this clearly and say how the discussion will take place and how agreements will be recorded. It is a good idea to display the timings on a sheet of paper and guide the participants verbally through the stages, for example, 'We're now on to the main item, discussion of the second version of our draft learning policy. Can we work for ten minutes in pairs, discussing and noting our main comments? Then we will go into our planning teams for 20 minutes and each team should try to come up with no more than five or six main points. Could they write these down on a piece of paper please? Then we can join together for another 20 minutes and discuss the points raised and for the final ten minutes we'll try to decide what we do next. Is everybody clear?'

● Always make time for a summary and conclusion at the end of the main item, focused on what has been decided and what is to be done next.

● Involving everybody in a discussion is a key chairing skill; however, this can often be done more effectively by designing a good process for a meeting rather than trying to make sure that everybody has a say.

In the previous process example, everybody starts off discussing in pairs so that even the shyest and most junior teacher gets a chance to say something. Breaking up big meetings into smaller discussion groups is a very useful way of increasing participation.

Follow-up

The chair should have the assistance of a minute-taker to record the key decisions. This has the additional advantage of having two people to check the agreements.

It's alright Neville's taking them down.

The minutes are slipping away . . .

Action-orientated minutes

Objective
To produce a brief record of a meeting which clearly lays out the agreements and decisions reached.

What you need
Photocopiable page 123.

What to do
Traditional, detailed minutes are a waste of time for busy teachers since all they require is a record of any agreements made and decisions reached about future action. The framework on photocopiable page 123 has been found useful in a wide variety of situations.

Action minutes

Meeting Whole staff	Attended by All staff present		Date 3/11/94	
Agenda item	Agreed points	Action	By whom	Deadline
1. Governors visit	Classes 5B and 2J to be visited	Governors to be briefed	John	Yesterday! (by Friday)
2. Learning Policy	Agreed changes recorded on flip chart.	Carol to update Draft 2, which is on the computer	Carol	15th Nov
3. Venue for staff party	We go to the Jolly Farmer!	Booking for 10 needed, set lunch	Jim to organise	20th Nov

The chair and minute-taker of a meeting should collaborate on the completion of the record. The temptation to do so during the meeting should be resisted – they need to be done from working notes taken during the meeting.

Follow-up
Circulate the minutes as quickly as possible. The starting point for the next meeting should be a check on who has agreed to do what and whether it has been done!

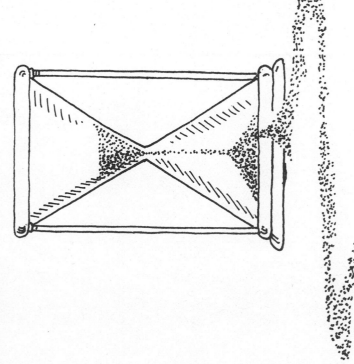

Time and the National Curriculum

The National Curriculum is making considerable demands upon primary teachers and the primary curriculum. The requirements put great pressure on teacher and classroom time; at the same time, teachers are expected to provide a broad and balanced curriculum, make accessible to all children the programmes of study and attainment targets, to assess the learning process systematically and to communicate the results of all these to parents and others. This chapter contains activities which should help teachers manage some of the necessary tasks as productively and time-efficiently as possible. They are arranged in three sections.

● Managing increased curriculum demands

The major concerns teachers have about the demands of the National Curriculum are the lack of time available to implement them and the speed of the implementation. Many of the activities in the previous chapters are appropriate to time-efficient implementation of the National Curriculum; this section contains activities provided specifically to help with increased curriculum demands when the time available has remained the same.

● Assessment and record-keeping

Teachers have always assessed children's learning – what is new about the current demands is the huge increase in the scope and scale of assessment requirements and the increased complexity of the documentation which supports it. There are few short cuts which can be recommended but it is important to think clearly about why something is being done and to weigh the time implications of assessment and record-keeping procedures with their likely outcomes in terms of information about children's learning.

● Reporting to parents

Informing parents and carers about children's learning has become a substantial task for teachers, especially as it is often necessary to do this and deploy the appropriate evidence on an individual basis. The suggestions here have been tried in schools and teachers have generally found them both effective and economical of time.

Managing increased curriculum demands

Progression and the National Curriculum

Objective
To make the maximum use of the National Curriculum's support for progression.

What you need
National Curriculum documents.

What to do
Examine some selected programmes of study and attainment targets as examples of progression. Follow through each individual example and think about how the different levels describe the development of understanding. There are some inconsistencies but also some examples of development which are extremely helpful to the class teacher. Good examples include the statement of attainment in historical understanding, in English. Progression is a very difficult issue for schools and teachers and the National Curriculum has been

helpful in focusing attention on this and in providing a progression structure in its requirements. The difficulties created by the National Curriculum are caused by too many requirements and not enough time rather than what it says about progression, which is supportive of effective learning and teaching and saves teachers reinventing the wheel!

Follow-up
Look at progression in the capacity for collaborative group work and independent learning. What is appropriate group work for children in Year 2 and what might you expect in Year 6? In Year 2, for instance, many children will be at the stage of working with one other child at a collaborative task; some will be able to work under supervision with two or three other children, perhaps painting a frieze. In Year 6, given regular experience of such work, children may well be able to undertake a variety of complex collaborative tasks, to understand some of the processes involved and to participate in a review of their work.

Staff discussion, both in planning teams and at whole-school level, is vital for thinking this through.

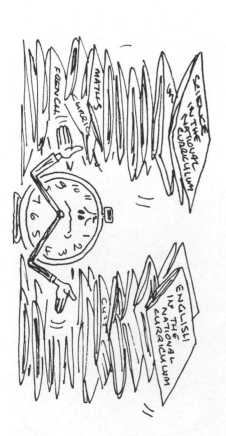

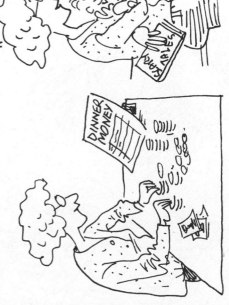

Routine classroom activities and the National Curriculum

Objective

To make clear the importance of routine classroom activities in fulfilling the requirements of the National Curriculum.

What you need

A list of your routine, ongoing classroom activities and processes.

What to do

Confronted with the National Curriculum requirements, it can sometimes seem to teachers that the whole curriculum they provide needs to be completely overhauled and that basic classroom routines and structures become less relevant. This is far from being the case. A brief analysis of your routines in the context

of the National Curriculum programmes of study and attainment targets will quickly make it clear that they play an essential part in implementation, especially in the core subjects. These basic routines include the following:

● maths scheme,
● handwriting and spelling practice,
● story time,
● skills practice, for example, mental arithmetic,
● counting the dinner money,
● discussing class news.

Do not be too quick to make changes in what has served you and your children well in the mistaken belief that the National Curriculum has changed everything!

Locating the National Curriculum requirements in what you currently do is as important as planning specifically for the National Curriculum. No teacher has the time to redesign their own curriculum from the ground up in response to the programmes of study and attainment targets and educationally it would be quite wrong to do so.

Cross-curricular learning activities

Objective

To use cross-curricular learning activities in implementing a part of the National Curriculum.

What you need

Cross-curricular learning activities; for example, a group designing and making a wheeled vehicle which can travel at least a metre under its own power.

What to do

Simple calculations will swiftly show that a ten-subject National Curriculum plus the cross-curricular skills, themes and dimensions cannot be delivered just through time-tabled subject teaching (and most teachers do not think even this would be an adequate curriculum). On practical, as well as educational, grounds some activities will have to be designed to combine several of the subjects.

In the example given above, the activity combines aspects of English, science, maths, technology and art. The time-saving aspect of cross-curricular learning activities, while being only one of the benefits, is highly relevant to the implementation of the National Curriculum.

Just as a ten-subject timetable in a primary school would be both inefficient in terms of time as well as being educationally unsatisfactory, the other extreme, of totally cross-curricular work, would be equally inadequate. Most teachers use a carefully planned blend of cross-curricular, skills-based and subject-organised teaching as appropriate. This seems to lead to the most effective use of time as well. A good rule of thumb, which corresponds well to the realities of a key stage 2 classroom, is to allocate around 40 per cent of classroom time to cross-curricular activities, leaving the other 60 per cent for single-subject and skills-based learning.

Unplanned learning

Objective

To be aware that learning can often be unplanned and seemingly unrelated to what the teacher has offered.

What you need

A broad view of learning and assessment which does not focus too tightly on what you have planned for the children.

What to do

How many teachers have taken children on a carefully planned trip only to find that the children's imagination has been caught by some trivial incidental detail such as the shape of the bus, someone they met or a tiny detail of an object they looked at? They are certainly learning, but sometimes the teacher wastes good learning time by trying to guide the children back to what has been planned for them; a wiser approach would be to make the most of their interest, however quirky. It is not a waste of time; on the contrary, focusing on such interests is often very productive in terms of achievement. Neither is the National Curriculum necessarily neglected if this is done!

Experienced teachers are skilled at reviewing these kinds of learning situations and in working out what learning has taken place. The important thing to remember is that the planned curriculum can eventually be returned to, whereas if time is wasted deflecting children from what they have seen in a situation, that moment of willingness and enthusiasm may well not come back again – motivated learners are effective learners. If the teacher, however unwittingly, gives the message that enthusiasm, imagination and motivation

have to wait their turn until something apparently more important has been covered, learning opportunities may be missed. The other point to bear in mind is that what the child is interested in may well be something which covers other aspects of the National Curriculum; as teachers become more familiar with the detail of the programmes of study and statements of attainment, they will get even better at recognising this and accept cheerfully that their planned learning activities will keep for another day.

Moderation and the National Curriculum

Objective
Consistency in meaning and application of attainment targets and programmes of study.

What you need
Arrangements for, and a willingness to discuss with colleagues the detail of the National Curriculum, especially the meaning and interpretation of the attainment targets and programmes of study.

What to do
Having effective informal systems of moderation for National Curriculum assessment can be a great time-saver for the individual teacher and there will probably be someone on the staff who can clarify a point instantly. Teachers working together in a planning group make a good moderation team; some schools also work closely with their core curriculum co-ordinators who provide a moderation service in a wider context than the individual subject area.

Choosing key elements of the National Curriculum

Objective

To identify and focus on the most important aspects of the National Curriculum.

What you need

A reminder for teachers about the need to identify and prioritise key aspects of the National Curriculum.

What to do

Look through the various orders to remind yourself of the main requirements – do this with a colleague if you can. What are the implications for classroom time? The classic example is Science AT1, which has the same weight in the final assessment as all the other Science ATs combined – is that reflected in your teaching? In

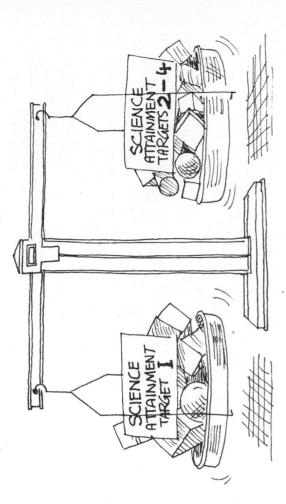

Start with one of the key attainment targets – in science, for instance. Bring along to your planning meeting examples of relevant classroom activities you have done and examples or notes of children's responses. The question to ask is 'At what level do I place this response and why?' Collective discussion will save a great deal of time in clearing up uncertainties and agreeing on interpretation. It will also promote the teacher's self-confidence in that her judgement has been discussed and supported by colleagues.

Follow-up

All these threads can be drawn together very effectively through a whole-school approach to the assessment and recording of learning. When this is linked to a whole-school planning approach, we really can save time and reduce stress.

English, is the balance of reading, writing, listening and speaking about right, bearing in mind the assessment requirements? Do we allocate too much time to the Numbers ATs compared with the others and is this justified?

Follow-up

Following an analysis like this, practical decisions have to be made about the allocation of classroom time. There is not enough time to manage all the requirements properly – given this fact, the best way to allocate time is through planned priorities.

Modular units of work

Objective

To cover statements of attainment efficiently, particularly in science.

What you need

Your planning framework and documentation.

What to do

While an integrated, topic-based approach to National Curriculum implementation can cover perhaps as much as a half of what needs to be done, a substantial amount of subject- and skill-based teaching is also necessary. Many teachers are now finding that a very efficient approach to some of the specific knowledge requirements, particularly in science, lies in planning and resourcing self-contained study modules usually, though not always, confined to a particular statement of attainment within a subject. They have found that the time, ingenuity and thought put into trying to find an

integrated approach/context to these statements of attainment can be a waste of time and may not lead to effective learning.

This modular approach usually involves two elements. A tightly focused, time-limited teaching programme which introduces the module goes alongside a 'resource box' of materials suitable for further exploration and investigation. Another approach is to use a set of structured tasks on workcards in conjunction with the resource material. The science programmes of study and statements of attainment on forces, and electricity and magnetism are two possibilities for such treatment.

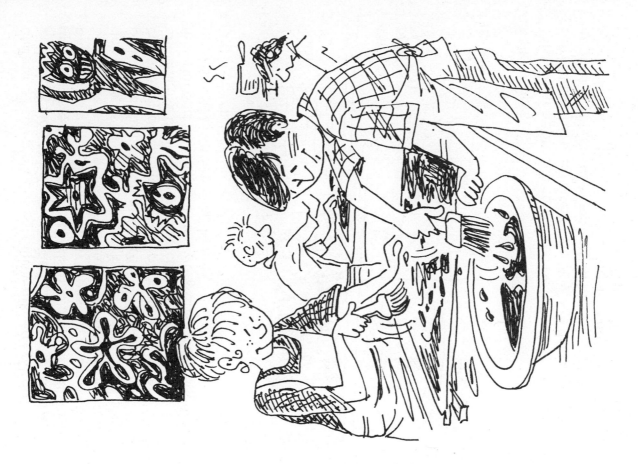

Blocks of time for the art curriculum

Objective

To make sure that children get specific art tuition and experiences, as well as opportunities for art within other curriculum areas and topic work.

What you need

Your teaching timetable; specific art experiences and techniques you wish to provide for the children.

What to do

Teachers are well versed in putting art at the service of the other curriculum areas – the superb displays in many primary classrooms are strong evidence of that. However, we are now required to go further – art is a National Curriculum subject with its own programmes of study and statements of attainment and will need to be assessed as a separate subject. There is concern among many teachers that the time and resource management of a high-quality art curriculum are already proving difficult. The following real-life example shows how to overcome some of those difficulties.

A Year 3 teacher I visited recently had been very concerned at the rather superficial nature of the art curriculum the children were experiencing and decided that the time and resource management issues needed confronting head-on. She decided that all the children should be given the opportunity to learn the skills of batik work and to work with another colleague who had these skills. She also wanted the children to have a finished product they could be proud of. The timetable was therefore drastically reorganised to block off two-

Assessment and record-keeping

Group presentations

Objective

To increase learning and to obtain assessment information from group presentations to other members of the class.

What you need

A collaborative activity, whose outcome could be presented by the group to the rest of the class.

What to do

Two key tasks in a primary classroom are to find effective ways for children to share what they have learned with other children and to assess individual learning within a collaborative group. Both these tasks can be undertaken at the same time through a group presentation to the other children. This can range from a simple account of what the group did to quite an extensive process involving self-assessment. For example, a group of children have been working on the sports page of the class newspaper. A group presentation of their work might include some of the following:

● Describing and presenting the outcome of the activity;
● Individuals describing their own contributions;
● The planning process — what collective decisions were made? How were tasks allocated?

and-a-half complete days for this work – a half-day skills workshop to be given by her colleague and a two-day intensive block for the children to do their individual batiks. This meant that the many materials needed could be collected and laid out for three days rather than a day or less – the children's work in progress could also be left undisturbed in the classroom. The teacher commented at the end that this approach was an efficient use of time and resources, both human and material and the quality of the work done was superior to what had been achieved before.

Follow-up

This sort of approach could well be followed in other curriculum areas, especially those where the activity involves a good deal of material and/or equipment which is difficult both to gather together and to get out/put away on a regular basis. To block off a day or more can be the most time-effective way of promoting quality through giving longer continuous access to materials.

● How well did the group work together? What would they do differently?

Any substantial collaborative learning activity should conclude with some sort of report back to the rest of the class, however informal. Teachers can provide or negotiate a structure for this, according to the age of the children and the degree of support required.

Follow-up

This report-back practice is often extended into a class assembly where the children have opportunities to communicate with a wider audience. This is another excellent source of assessment information for teachers.

Planning assessment into activities

Objective

To make planning for assessment an integral part of curriculum planning.

What you need

You may find the chart on photocopiable page 124 useful, although many other starting points are possible.

What to do

When you plan learning activities for your children, a brief consideration of how the intended learning might be assessed will save time later. Assessment opportunities often arise in the course of the activity and this needs some advance thought and planning, especially in relation to the aspects of the National

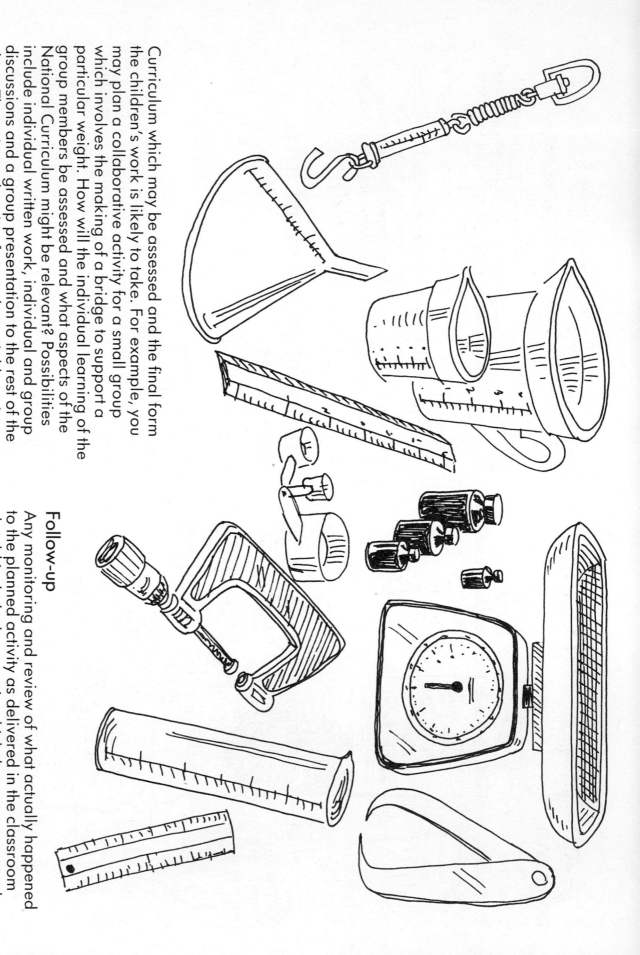

Curriculum which may be assessed and the final form the children's work is likely to take. For example, you may plan a collaborative activity for a small group which involves the making of a bridge to support a particular weight. How will the individual learning of the group members be assessed and what aspects of the National Curriculum might be relevant? Possibilities include individual written work, individual and group discussions and a group presentation to the rest of the class. The written planning for a substantial learning activity like this should include a note of the proposed assessment methods.

Follow-up

Any monitoring and review of what actually happened to the planned activity as delivered in the classroom should include the ways in which the assessment took place. Did you find any evidence of learning and through what means?

specifically relate to forces and energy. Such evidence is perfectly acceptable for National Curriculum assessment purposes.

If you are short of time and realise that you are not going to be able to cover everything you have planned, it may be best to look for evidence in this indirect way rather than hastily construct a teaching programme which will cover the missing parts – this may be a poor use of time.

The nature and extent of evidence

Objective
To use reasonable professional judgement in the assessment process.

What you need
No special requirements.

What to do
A good deal of time and effort can go into trying to be certain when making National Curriculum assessments. Some teachers set such high standards of evidence that they find this working against their own professional judgement of a child's level of knowledge. An assessment is only a 'snapshot' taken at a particular time and place. It can easily change at a later date without this being inconsistent. Time can be saved and stress avoided by not insisting on 'courtroom' standards of proof of knowledge and trusting your professional

I haven't taught it so I can't assess it!

Objective
To clarify the problem of whether it is possible to assess a particular aspect of the National Curriculum when it has not been covered by your class.

What you need
No special requirements.

What to do
Even if you have not taught something directly, there are indirect methods of assessing the knowledge children have acquired about it in other ways. You might, for instance, find evidence of children's understanding of forces or energy through activities such as PE, model making or individual and group discussion, even though you have not provided learning activities which

Assessment through group discussion

Objective

To use time more efficiently by assessing individual learning through outcomes of group activity.

What you need

A group which has completed a collaborative task.

What to do

Ask the group to tell you about what they have done and then take the opportunities offered to question individuals about their own contributions, both directly and indirectly. This can be a very natural process and levels of understanding often become very apparent. This process is also supportive of the less able child.

The product of the activity may also include individual contributions of written and other work, for example, a specific contribution to a model or a written-up account. These, of course, provide valuable assessment material.

The following transcript is based on a recent observation made in a Year 2 class. The teacher is looking for information about children's understanding of what a fair test is and also about their speaking and listening. The three children were testing how far different toy cars would travel if released at the top of a slope – in this case a large triangular building brick.

judgement and knowledge of the child.

Evidence of learning is a complex issue and it is not an easy thing for individual teachers to get to grips with by themselves.

When you come to make National Curriculum assessment judgements, keep these factors in mind and do not waste time trying for impossible standards.

Teacher: Children, come and tell me about what you did. John, you start.

John: We let the car go . . . and it rolled down . . . it went far . . .

Teacher: How far, John?

John: Very far . . .

Aziz: Miss, John didn't start his car at the top . . . I did and it goes further if you do that.

Gary: I put the brick on the carpet and my car stopped quickly, didn't it, Aziz?

Aziz: Yeah, Gary, but it wasn't the same car . . . .

John: It was my car . . . my go!

Teacher: All right, John . . . Aziz, why should you use the same car?

Aziz: Well . . . different ones go different . . . you have to use the same one . . . .

Teacher: But I said you could use several cars, Aziz . . .

Aziz: No, miss, I mean if you want to try it on the carpet and on the floor, you have to use the same car . . . it's not fair if you don't.

Gary: And another thing, miss, you have to start the car at the same place on the brick . . . .

Teacher: How did you do that, Gary?

Gary: I put the back wheels right on the edge of the brick so it was the same every time . . . .

Teacher: What was the same?

Gary: Where they [the cars] started from. And the floor or the carpet has to be the same, you shouldn't change it in the middle . . .

87

Using individual observation cards

Objective

To use time efficiently by gathering and recording some assessment data during the school day.

What you need

An index card for every child in the class; a container for the cards (these can be bought or a small box can be suitably adapted).

What to do

Write a child's name on each card. Start with the child on the first card and for a whole day try to be especially aware of that particular child as a learner, within the normal context of what is happening in the class. Write down any points you feel are worth recording on the index card. Keep the card box accessible so that notes can often be made very soon after the observation. Try to concentrate on learning aspects rather than social comments.

It is not being suggested here that a teacher should spend the whole day on constant observation of only one child – this is quite impracticable. However, by taking odd moments during the day to observe and take notes, a surprising amount of information can be gathered.

The next convenient day, put the first card at the back of the pile, take the next one and so on.

Use the information on the cards as a supplement to your main record-keeping system and as a source of assessment information.

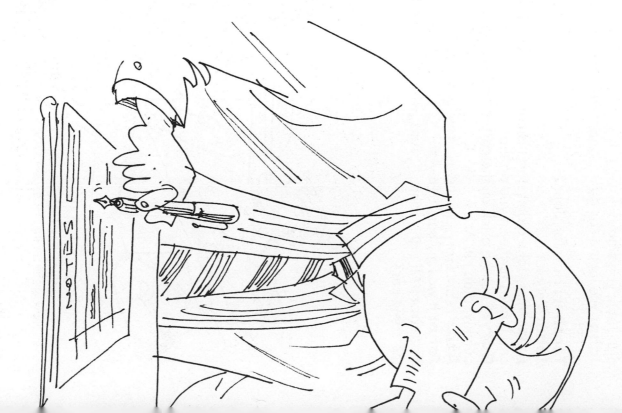

Keeping samples of children's work

Objective
To support the assessment of learning by keeping repesentative samples of children's work.

What you need
A framework and guidance for collecting samples of children's work; somewhere to put them.

What to do
Ideally, the collection of work samples should be placed in the context of a whole-school approach to assessment. It is even better when that approach is through a record of achievement. Whole-school approaches do save a lot of time for the class teacher.

Follow-up
You may wish to continue using this system on a selective basis as suggested above. You could also try using it systematically to assess all the children over a four-week period.

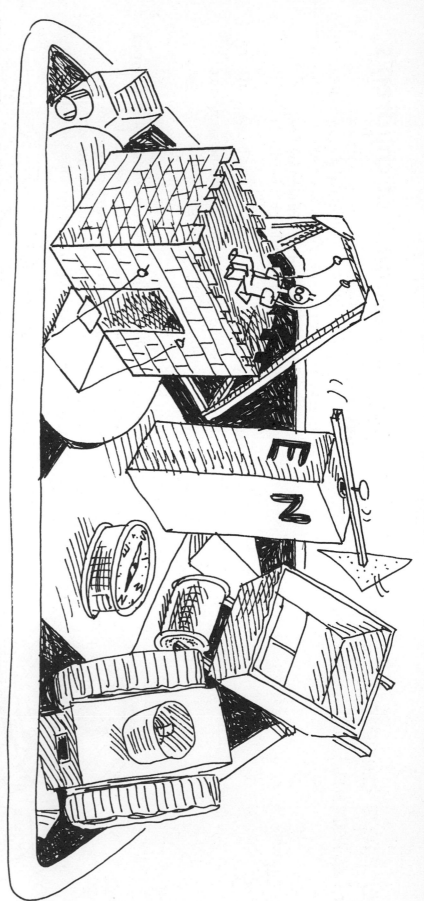

However, if you do have to 'invent your own wheel', make a start by keeping one or two representative dated examples for each child which you feel show that child's achievement most fairly. Storage is a real problem for most teachers. It is restricting to start with work which fits a standard A4 file, but it is better than nothing.

Criteria for collection need to be agreed collectively, otherwise much time is wasted by individual teachers making individual decisions. The following questions may be useful when deciding on the criteria.

- Is it to be a piece of language work or will other subjects be included?
- How often will work be collected from each child?
- Is it normal classroom work or something done specifically as a work sample?
- How much do presentation and neatness matter?
- What will be done with the samples?
- Is it 'best' or 'representative' work?
- Will the children be involved in what is chosen?
- Is it to be unaided work only? What does 'unaided' mean?

Follow-up

The storage of two-dimensional work presents many problems, but a whole new set of issues arise when three-dimensional work is involved. Perhaps we need another solution altogether (see the following activity).

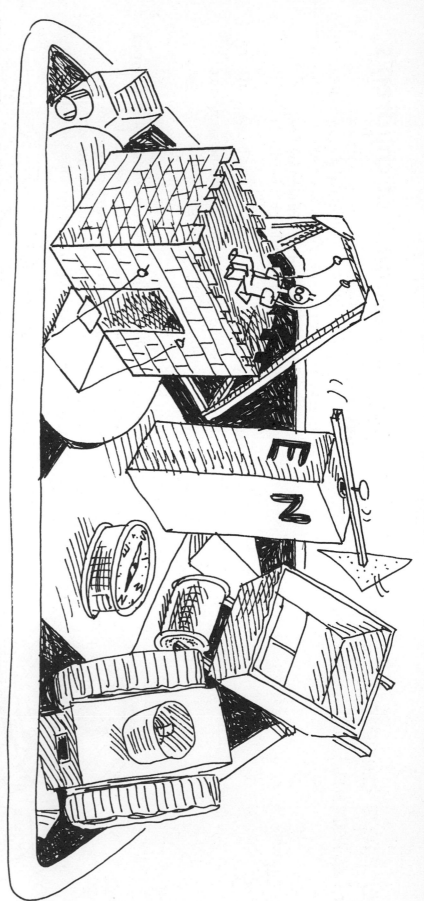

Using a camera in the classroom

Objective
To document and record the work of children, both individually and in groups.

What you need
A 35mm compact camera with a built-in flash (absolutely essential), automatic exposure and autofocus. (Every school should have one as an essential piece of educational equipment.)

What to do
Classroom assessment for the busy teacher is challenging and difficult to make time for. In particular, a range of evidence now needs to be taken into account besides the traditional variety of written work in the exercise books and work on the walls. The results of group activity are a good example – it is often just not practicable to store a model, yet some sort of a record is often invaluable for assessment purposes, as it is easy to forget what the children did.

The 'point and snap' cameras are ideal for taking flash pictures in the classroom of all kinds of children's work. Items at various stages of completion can be recorded, especially model making and other three-dimensional work. Creative arts work of various kinds can also be recorded. Photographs are also invaluable for discussions with individual or groups of children, reminding them vividly of what they did and stimulating further discussion. A camera is a key tool for supporting assessment, particularly in areas which are not amenable to recording in traditional pencil and paper ways.

Compared with written recording, a photograph saves a lot of time, not only in assessment but also, in some circumstances, in reporting to parents. The cost of the film needs to be set against the teacher-time cost in having to make a written record.

Follow-up

These cameras are so simple that they can be used by even quite young children with a minimum of supervision. It is certainly feasible to allow groups or individuals the opportunity to photograph their own work as part of the record-keeping process.

Time implications of Science Attainment Target 1

Objective
To allocate time appropriately for Science AT1.

What you need
Your planning framework and documentation.

What to do
Attainment Target 1 in Science counts for 50 per cent in the final assessment in both Key Stages 1 and 2. All the other statements of attainment together count for the remaining 50 per cent but teachers often do not see the time implications of this. This is probably because AT1 is a process AT, whereas the rest are content-based. What can happen is that the planning concentrates heavily on covering the content, and tends to leave the process to take care of itself. A better approach, both educationally and from a time management point of view, would be to try to deliver the content through the scientific process as much as possible, which would mean AT1 was regularly covered, as it should be, given its importance. Allied to this should be a realisation that any one individual content AT is of little significance in terms of the final assessment. It is very poor time management to concentrate too much on any one of these to the detriment of the others, and even worse if this leads to neglect of Science AT1.

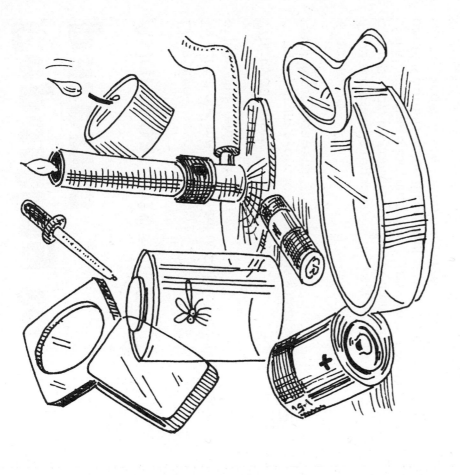

Follow-up
There is a welcome tendency now to 'map' attainment targets across the whole of a key stage, that is to plan in advance the year in which they are going to be covered. If this is done, time should also be allocated to 'revisit' them briefly for each child in the last year of the key stage for final assessment purposes and to confirm or revise levels in the light of new evidence. This does not necessarily mean covering them again in class – it is a checking and monitoring device for individual children.

Reporting to parents

Asking parents

Objective

To collect and make efficient use of parental knowledge of their children's learning.

What you need

A regular framework for doing this which suits you and the children's parents.

What to do

If you see parents regularly at the beginning and end of a school day, try consciously to ask them about aspects of their children's learning which you are not clear about – parents value this greatly if they feel you really want to know. More formal meetings, such as parents' evenings, should always include a section where the teacher asks questions rather than gives out information.

Follow-up

Further developments might include Parent Conferencing, a concept developed by the ILEA Primary Learning Record, where you systematically ask parents about their child's learning experience at home (see the activity on page 60).

Informing parents

Objective
To increase parents' knowledge of the National Curriculum.

What you need
Photocopiable page 125.

What to do
Experience has shown that even well-informed parents are not very clear about how the National Curriculum relates to what actually happens in the classroom. Instead of frequent – and sometimes stressful – conversations with individual parents, why not try giving parents a copy of the termly summary sheet shown on photocopiable page 125? This could be also incorporated into a newsletter (see page 62).

PARENTS EVENING

NATIONAL CURRICULUM THE WHINGES

PLEASE TAKE ONE

NATIONAL CURRICULUM THE FACTS

MR JONES

Follow-up

Parents want to know how they can help at home and are especially keen if they feel they are helping with National Curriculum work. There are quite a few possibilities here for the resourceful teacher, although the giving of National Curriculum homework is not recommended!

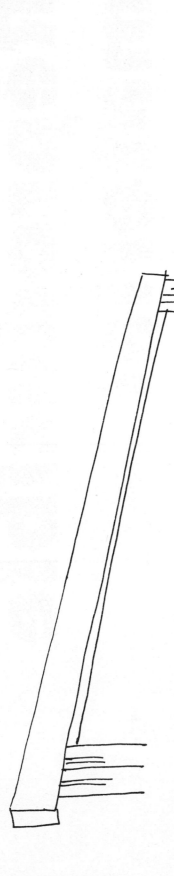

Annual report to parents

Objective
To report progress and achievement to parents as clearly as possible.

What you need
Photocopiable page 126.

What to do
There is now a legal requirement to report annually to parents about the progress of their child and this should include reported National Curriculum results at the end of Year 2 and Year 6 (the latter from July 1994). This is an important opportunity to talk about achievement of individual children. If the school believes in a wide interpretation of achievement, perhaps to include social and problem-solving aspects, then the annual report should include information on these. It would be important, both from a consistency and time-saving point of view, for the whole staff to agree a format for this reporting and photocopiable page 126 could be a starting point, in conjunction with the new reporting requirements recently announced (August 1992).

Reproducible material

Time analysis: a typical week, see page 7

Time analysis

Total time in school (A) =

LESS   Official lunchtime
        Morning break
        Afternoon break =

Unofficial extensions of
lunch/breaktime (estimate) =

Registration/dinner money collection =

Time spent getting to and from
assemblies, swimming, games, etc. =

Other interruptions in lesson time =

Total time losses (B) =

Time remaining (A) − (B) =

Hrs   min

This page may be photocopied for use in the classroom and should not be declared in any return in respect of any photocopying licence.

Out-of-class time-log, see page 8

Out-of-class time-log

Possible categories might be: preparation, marking, reading, record-keeping, collaborative planning, postholder work, mounting and displaying work, meetings, school clubs, etc. — try to have no more than five or six categories for your log. Another way of using the log is to write a short description of your out-of-school activities for each day and estimate how long they take.

Total out-of-class/ out-of-school hours

Days	Categories					Hours worked
Mon						
Tue						
Wed						
Thu						
Fri						
Sat						
Sun						

This page may be photocopied for use in the classroom and should not be declared in any return in respect of any photocopying licence.

Task batching sheet, see page 15

People to contact	Done	Things to write	Done	Things to obtain	Done	Other tasks	Done

This page may be photocopied for use in the classroom and should not be declared in any return in respect of any photocopying licence.

This page may be photocopied for use in the classroom and should not be declared in any return in respect of any photocopying licence.

Comments

Arrival in school	
Arrival in class	
Assemblies	
Playground duty	
PE/Hall lessons	
Appointments	

Make an honest appraisal of your punctuality record in relation to the above categories. The following comments may be useful as a guide.

- I make a point of being on time for this.

- I usually manage to get there on time.

- I try to be on time but often have problems achieving this.

- I am on time when I feel like making a special effort.

- I don't really bother what time I arrive for this unless under pressure.

- I never ever bother being on time for this.

Bring forward file, see page 22

Date	Document	Action needed

Bring forward file

Contents

This page may be photocopied for use in the classroom and should not be declared in any return in respect of any photocopying licence.

Course and professional reading log, see page 28

Course and professional reading log

Course title/reference and date	Points to remember	Date	Comments, thoughts and reflections

This page may be photocopied for use in the classroom and should not be declared in any return in respect of any photocopying licence.

What I need tomorrow, see page 29

What I need tomorrow

Week starting	
For Monday	
For Tuesday	
For Wednesday	
For Thursday	
For Friday	

This page may be photocopied for use in the classroom and should not be declared in any return in respect of any photocopying licence.

This page may be photocopied for use in the classroom and should not be declared in any return in respect of any photocopying licence.

Preferred learning styles, see page 42

Preferred learning styles

Class

Date	Name of child	Preferred style(s) — examples/evidence

This page may be photocopied for use in the classroom and should not be declared in any return in respect of any photocopying licence.

This page may be photocopied for use in the classroom and should not be declared in any return in respect of any photocopying licence.

TV/radio programmes to be recorded

Class

	Programme details: title/time/channel
Monday	
Tuesday	
Wednesday	
Thursday	
Friday	
Saturday/Sunday	

Topic work record sheet, see page 48

Topic work record sheet

Year [ ]

Class [ ]

	Topic title	Comments – reaction of children, National Curriculum delivery, main learning outcomes, etc.
Autumn	Topic title	
	Topic title	
Spring	Topic title	
	Topic title	
Summer	Topic title	
	Topic title	

This page may be photocopied for use in the classroom and should not be declared in any return in respect of any photocopying licence.

The planning cycle, see page 51

The planning cycle

1. The task

Everyone in the group must understand what the task is.

Is the task clear to everyone?

2. The plan – how are we going to do it?

What are we hoping to end up with?

What needs to be done?

What things will be needed?

Who will do what?

When will it be done?

3. Doing what we have planned.

Who monitors this?

How do we change parts of the plan if necessary?

4. The review

What went well?

What did not go so well?

What will we do differently next time?

This page may be photocopied for use in the classroom and should not be declared in any return in respect of any photocopying licence.

Self-evaluation sheet, see page 52

Self-evaluation sheet

| Name | | Class | | Date | |

What I did

What did I do/learn well?

What did I do/learn not so well?

What do I need to do next?

This page may be photocopied for use in the classroom and should not be declared in any return in respect of any photocopying licence.

This page may be photocopied for use in the classroom and should not be declared in any return in respect of any photocopying licence.

Group work evaluation sheet

Names

What did you do together?

What did you do separately?

What were you pleased about in your work?

What were you not so pleased about?

My weekly record sheet, see page 54

My weekly record sheet

Name

Week beginning

The main things I did:

The main things I learned:

My thoughts about next week:

This page may be photocopied for use in the classroom and should not be declared in any return in respect of any photocopying licence.

This page may be photocopied for use in the classroom and should not be declared in any return in respect of any photocopying licence.

Part-time teacher help analysis, see page 57

Part-time teacher help analysis

The present situation in my class

Current help

How is it used?

How effective is it?

My preferred situation

What help do I really need?

How should this be related
to children's learning needs?

How will we plan/liaise together?

Reasons for my preferred situation

Do these include promoting
children's learning? How would it?

What would I do differently
(especially timewise) if I had extra help?

The changes that need to be made

What do these changes mean for me?
For the children?

What do I have to do now?

Summary of agreed tasks/planning, see page 58

Class		Summary of agreed tasks/planning
	Person and time	
Mon		
Tues		
Wed		
Thurs		
Fri		

This page may be photocopied for use in the classroom and should not be declared in any return in respect of any photocopying licence.

This page may be photocopied for use in the classroom and should not be declared in any return in respect of any photocopying licence.

Activity information sheet

Date and time	Name

Children involved

Activity

Materials required

What to do

Comments

Donated-time register

Name	What is offered	Time available	Contact details

This page may be photocopied for use in the classroom and should not be declared in any return in respect of any photocopying licence.

This page may be photocopied for use in the classroom and should not be declared in any return in respect of any photocopying licence.

Parents' evening record sheet

Class   Date

Appt Time	Name of child	Points to raise with parent(s)/carer(s)	Points raised by parent(s)/carer(s)

Class . . . Newsletter

Date

What we are doing in class

How you can help

Materials we need

Personal news/birthdays etc.

Future events

This page may be photocopied for use in the classroom and should not be declared in any return in respect of any photocopying licence.

This page may be photocopied for use in the classroom and should not be declared in any return in respect of any photocopying licence.

Collaborative planning meeting

Date   Present

Agreed that . . .	Action by whom and when

Meeting planning sheet, see page 66

Meeting planning sheet   **Date**

Why have the meeting?

Purposes   What outcomes are required?

1.
2.
3.

Draft agenda Keep the number of items to a minimum.

1.
2.
3.

Main item: how will it be dealt with?

Meeting administration

Where?   When?   Who?

Materials needed

Anything else?

This page may be photocopied for use in the classroom and should not be declared in any return in respect of any photocopying licence.

This page may be photocopied for use in the classroom and should not be declared in any return in respect of any photocopying licence.

Meeting:

Date:

Place:

Start:

Finish:

Main purpose:

Please bring:

Agenda:

Notes:

Action minutes, see page 71

Action minutes

Meeting	Attended by		Date	

Agenda item	Agreed points	Action	By whom	Deadline

This page may be photocopied for use in the classroom and should not be declared in any return in respect of any photocopying licence.

Planning assessment into activities, see page 83

Activity	Subjects and ATs	Intended learning	Assessment procedures

This page may be photocopied for use in the classroom and should not be declared in any return in respect of any photocopying licence.

Parents' information sheet, see page 95

Parents' information sheet

Date   Class

What we are doing now

How this relates to the National Curriculum

How you can help at home

This page may be photocopied for use in the classroom and should not be declared in any return in respect of any photocopying licence.

This page may be photocopied for use in the classroom and should not be declared in any return in respect of any photocopying licence.

Annual report to parents

Name   Age   Date

Attendance

Progress and achievements (including National Curriculum)

Areas for special attention next year

Other Scholastic books

Bright Ideas

The *Bright Ideas* books provide a wealth of resources for busy primary school teachers. There are now more than 40 titles published, providing clearly explained and illustrated ideas on topics ranging from *Writing* and *Maths Activities* to *Assemblies* and *Christmas Art and Craft*. Each book contains material which can be photocopied for use in the classroom.

Bright Ideas for Early Years

The *Bright Ideas for Early Years* series has been written specifically for the unique needs of nursery and reception teachers, playgroup leaders and all those who work with very young children.

Each title has 96 pages of illustrated early years information, providing an excellent foundation for later National Curriculum work.

The books provide sound, practical advice on all areas of learning, together with original activities which have been specially designed to develop essential early childhood skills.

Inspirations

The *Inspirations* series offers the same winning *Bright Ideas* philosophy of activity-centred learning, plus thoughtful and supportive advice on using these activities within the framework of the National Curriculum.

This is an ideal series for teachers who want ideas for classroom activities, but who also welcome extra information on curriculum content, assessment, recording, teaching strategies and delivery.

Scholastic Collections

Scholastic Collections is a stylish and highly original new series for primary teachers. Containing a large proportion of specially commissioned material, it has been designed for those who need an accessible collection of songs, poems, rhymes, games and plays to fit in with a particular topic.

Each contains line drawings which bring the material to life, while the beautifully illustrated covers reflect the spirit of the selections.

Management Books

The *Management Books* are designed to help teachers to organise their time, classroom and teaching more efficiently. The books deal with topical issues, such as *Parents and Schools* and organising and planning *Project Teaching*, and are written by authors with lots of practical advice and experience to share.